Anticipating Change
Secrets Behind the SAP™ Empire

Send Us Your Comments:

To comment on this book or any other PRIMA TECH title, visit our reader response page on the Web at **www.prima-tech.com/comments**.

How to Order:

For information on quantity discounts, contact the publisher: Prima Publishing, P.O. Box 1260BK, Rocklin, CA 95677-1260; (916) 787-7000. On your letterhead, include information concerning the intended use of the books and the number of books you want to purchase.

Anticipating Change
Secrets Behind the SAP™ Empire

Hasso Plattner in conversation with
August-Wilhelm Scheer,
Siegfried Wendt,
and Daniel S. Morrow

Translated from the German by William McKone

A Division of Prima Publishing

A Division of Prima Publishing

Prima Publishing and colophon are registered trademarks of Prima Communications, Inc. PRIMA TECH is a trademark of Prima Communications, Inc., Roseville, California 95661.

SAP is a registered trademark of SAP Aktiengesellschaft, Systems, Applications, and Products in Data Processing, Neurottstrasse 16, 69190 Walldorf, Germany. The publisher gratefully acknowledges SAP's kind permission to use its trademark in this publication. SAP AG is not the publisher of this book and is not responsible for it under any aspect of press law.

R/2, R/3, and SAPPHIRE are either trademarks or registered trademarks of SAP Aktiengesellschaft, Walldorf, Germany.

Prima Publishing and the author have attempted throughout this book to distinguish proprietary trademarks from descriptive terms by following the capitalization style used by the manufacturer.

Information contained in this book has been obtained by Prima Publishing from sources believed to be reliable. However, because of the possibility of human or mechanical error by our sources, Prima Publishing, or others, the Publisher does not guarantee the accuracy, adequacy, or completeness of any information and is not responsible for any errors or omissions or the results obtained from use of such information. Readers should be particularly aware of the fact that the Internet is an ever-changing entity. Some facts may have changed since this book went to press.

Library of Congress Catalog Card Number: 00-103487

Library of Congress Cataloging-in-Publication Data on File

ISBN: 0-7615-2913-6
00 01 02 03 04 HH 10 9 8 7 6 5 4 3 2 1
Printed in the United States of America

Contents

Preface

By Dr. Thomas Middelhoff,
Chairman of the Board of Bertelsmann AG

The business history of SAP is one of the most exciting stories of the past 20 years, and Hasso Plattner is one of the most notable business personalities in Germany. This is rich material for a good book.

In the beginning, the business from Walldorf was a typical start-up, a small software company with much larger competition: IBM, Siemens, Lotus, and Microsoft. Today, SAP is a showpiece business with worldwide activities. There can be only one answer to the question of whether a business outside the US has a chance to reach the top going against the market and strength of the American software companies: Yes. Look at the example of SAP.

SAP has achieved this success with flat hierarchies, an "honest business culture" (according to Plattner), a close customer orientation, and a clear goal of going to America and being successful there. SAP makes 40 percent of its sales in the US and 20 percent in Germany.

How the stories resemble each other! German businesses that have aggressively pursued globalization are often successful; where they have waited and timidly watched the new competition, they have been pushed to the side. At Bertelsmann, we also have taken this to heart, and today no media firm is more international than we are. Besides globalization, the Internet is the next big challenge for businesses in all branches of the economy. Prices will be transparent, markets global, work processes digital, and changes will happen more rapidly. All areas of business must examine their structures, constantly adjust them, and stay flexible. Only those who are nimble and integrate the

Internet into their own basic business will remain large. Those showing the way, and the big winners of this development, are the multimedia start-ups with their unimaginable stock capitalization; they are doing an end run around the traditional branches and catching up with or overtaking the classic large businesses. AOL's takeover of Time Warner in January 2000 is the most notable proof of this thesis.

Hasso Plattner tells a good story about an American colleague who warned, "Keep an eye on the Internet" at a time when hardly anyone in Germany was talking about it. In fact, many businesses for a long time underrated this dramatic transformation in the companies and branches brought about by this technology, and some are still doing it today. SAP reacted with mySAP.com, and Bertelsmann is today better prepared for these challenges with its Internet and e-commerce activities than any other media enterprise in the world.

There is a "war for talent," that is, a competition by the top businesses for those people who have embraced both the inevitability of globalization and the Internet world in thought and behavior. The key, says Hasso Plattner, is simply enjoying the work and working as part of the team— a statement that is as simple as it is fascinating. The stock options are certainly important, but they are not everything. Leaders want to move something—themselves and the company—and they are seeking challenges. They want to identify their work with the product. What they avoid is operating under the principles "We have always done it this way" or "As the new guy, you first have to take your place at the back of the line."

The law of the Internet world is "Put everything up for examination." Yes, we need continuity, but react swiftly. Businesses such as SAP or Bertelsmann are, and will continue in a global economy to be, magnets for creative and entrepreneurial talent, which will keep them innovative and top-ranked on a world level. For me, this is one of the central concepts of this informative book.

Foreword

This book was an adventure. The material was recorded in six lively discussion sessions and then revised editorially. The initial concept of equally dividing the content between the three partners in the conversations—Plattner, Scheer, and Wendt—was discarded early on. The stories from Hasso Plattner proved to be so exciting that the other partners in the discussions, Scheer and Wendt, concentrated more on motivating Hasso Plattner and maintaining continuity through their questions and contributions.

This format was the origin of the fascinating documentation of the founding and development of SAP AG, the essential milestones of the R/3 system, and the forward-thinking strategy of SAP. The text describes the transition from the R/2 system to the R/3 system and the development of mySAP.com in a particularly impressive way. Although the first change in generations was more technically based and somewhat followed the trend from the central computer to the client/server architecture, the development of mySAP.com is associated with a new concept in business administration processes. As Plattner says in connection with this development, "SAP was founded anew."

Many of the statements are interesting far beyond the sphere of SAP. They describe the atmosphere in the high-tech world, the aggressive behavior of the market participants, and the enormous demands on mental flexibility and physical stamina.

Even though the individual discussion sessions had previously selected themes and are introduced by captions, they evolved spontaneously. The intensity of the discussions reflects the wide-ranging, word-for-word reconstruction of the sessions. The publisher's editors have succeeded in preserving the dynamics and atmosphere of the talks. In the remarks about technical problems, they paid more attention to the content being clear than to the accuracy of usage of technical terms.

This book thus provides an important picture of the thought processes of one of the most important creators of the software industry. We hope you will experience the openness, involvement, and mental power that we had as partners in the discussions with Hasso Plattner.

August-Wilhelm Scheer
Saarbrücken, January 2000

Siegfried Wendt
Potsdam, January 2000

Acknowledgments

Many people contributed to making this an exciting and informative book; my thanks to all of them.

My first acknowledgment belongs to my two partners in the conversations, Prof. Dr. August-Wilhelm Scheer and Prof. Dr. Siegfried Wendt. They had the idea and convinced me to join this venture. They constantly kept me motivated, one urging on the other, with a lot of discussion—sometimes controversial and provocative, but always constructive. The adventure of this book would not have happened without them. Sincere thanks also to Dr. Thomas Middelhoff, Chairman of the Board of Bertelsmann AG, for his willingness to open this book with his preface.

This book is inseparably connected with the past, present, and future of SAP. Without SAP, there would not have been a book to publish. Without my four founding colleagues, there would have been no SAP—at least not as it is now, as successful as it is. I therefore dedicate this book to Dietmar Hopp, Klaus E. Tschira, Hans-Werner Hector, and Claus Wellenreuther for the boldness, time, courage, and personal sacrifice they made to invest in a vision. I include their families in my gratitude!

Decisive energy also came from my four colleagues on the board at that time, all of whom have accompanied me for a long time. My special thanks go to Henning Kagermann, Peter Zencke, Claus E. Heinrich, and Gerhard Oswald. The success of SAP from the very first years right up until today is largely thanks to them. They effected developments and moved them forward. Likewise, I thank all past and present

employees of SAP throughout the world for their commitment and the work they have done together in such a productive manner.

I further thank Dipl-Hdl Michael Hoffmann and Dipl-
Wirtsch-Ing Markus Bold for their preparation of the
discussion agendas, as well as the editorial revision of
the manuscripts and technical remarks; Lucie Bender and
Vera Griesser for their careful entry of the text; as well as
Bernd-Uwe Pagel and Bernhard Hochlehnert of SAP AG
for their positive and constructive collaboration on this
project. I also thank The Galileo Press publishing house,
and in particular Mr. Tomas Wehren for their professional
cooperation.

Finally, my thanks also go to David K. Allison of the Smithsonian Institution, National Museum of American History,
Division of Information Technology, for permission to print
in this book the interview that Daniel S. Morrow conducted
with me in April 1997.

Hasso Plattner
Walldorf, January 2000

Hasso Plattner, chairman of SAP America, Inc., vice chairman of the board of SAP AG, and the chief architect of the R/3 system, received the 1997 Information Technology Leadership Award for Global Integration as part of the Computerworld Smithsonian Awards program. Dr. Plattner was honored with this award at the National Building Museum in Washington, D.C., on June 9, 1997.

The following interview took place as part of the Smithsonian's program to capture oral histories for posterity. It was conducted in English. Dr. Plattner's partner in the conversation was Daniel S. Morrow, executive director of the Smithsonian Awards.

Chapter 1

The Luck of the Capable

From the beginning, it was our idea that everyone could do everything at once. You would have access to current information wherever you were and could get everything that you wanted to know. We had to struggle for years on end. People debated this and said that it is not the right way of looking at things.

Now that has changed because of the Internet.

Walldorf, April 9, 1997

MORROW On behalf of the Smithsonian Institution and the future generations of students and scholars and citizens of the world for whom we hold these documents in trust, and on behalf of Dr. David Spielberg and his colleagues at Ernst & Young, whose generosity makes this program possible, I congratulate you on 25 years of success with SAP, on the quality of your work, and your contributions to global integration. I thank you for this time and this contribution to the history of information technology.

PLATTNER Thank you very much. It's a great honor for me that this interview is taking place, especially because I'm the first non-American to receive this honor.

MORROW Let's begin by talking about your birthplace, your family, and your early education before you went to Karlsruhe.

Origins

PLATTNER I was born in Berlin. My father was and is a medical doctor, and I spent the first 15 years in Berlin. Then I went to Bavaria, which was quite a move—somewhat like moving from New York to Houston. I spent some time in Bavaria. I went to school in Switzerland for three years, then started my studies in "elektrotechnik" in Karlsruhe. When I graduated with a degree in "elektrotechnik," I joined IBM.

MORROW "Elektrotechnik" has been translated in English as "communications engineering." Isn't it more equivalent to an electrical engineering degree?

PLATTNER In those days, it was a combination of electrical engineering and computer technology. Between 1965 and 1968, all I studied was digital communications, and in the last years of my education, I focused on software.

Personal
influences **MORROW** When you were a young man, before you went to university, who were some of the greatest influences on your life and career?

PLATTNER My grandfather was a great influence on me. For 11 years, I was not able to communicate with him because he was a prisoner of war. He happened to have the same name, Funk, as the German Minister for Work who had been responsible for some of the atrocities of the government, so he had 11 years of trouble because of his name. He was an engineer and a technical director. Perhaps from him I got my engineering attitude, a sense of what engineering is about, and my perfectionism.

Another influence was my father, who is a medical doctor. Again, perfectionism is perhaps one of my worst traits.

MORROW Some of your colleagues who have won this award have told us stories of things they did in their youth that were sort of giveaways about their future careers. Steve Jobs, for example, said that he had a teacher who actually motivated him to do his course work by paying him $5 to finish his math homework.

John Warnock at Adobe Systems was actually failing mathematics until one of his teachers transformed his whole attitude toward math and made his career possible. Was there a teacher who was an inspiration to you early on?

PLATTNER Two teachers inspired me early on. One of my teachers in West Berlin had just come from East Berlin. He was my teacher for arts. He made the statement, "When you reach the point that you don't change your mind any more, you know you're old." That idea really stuck with me. I still think about it. Whenever I start feeling very conservative, or get stuck in a specific situation, that idea comes to mind. So far, it has motivated me to find loopholes, get out of being stuck, and change my mind.

A maxim for life

The other teacher who had a great influence on me taught at Lake Constance, where I went to school the last three years. I lived in Switzerland—my mother lived in Switzerland—and he was my math and physics teacher. He had been a seaman for 10 years before becoming a teacher. Although he was a seaman, he came back to teach math and physics. That was an unusual combination.

MORROW Was that the origin of your interest in sailing?

PLATTNER No. My father and I sailed when we lived in Berlin. We had no money—nothing—but even in the deepest depression, at the time when Berlin was a real island and we had the big airlift, we had a sailboat. Even though I was very little, I remember the airlift of 1948. I remember the British seaplanes coming in, landing close to the boat.

As a student, I was already a businessman. I was a relatively good student, with some flaws. Once, I got a very bad grade in French, so I told my French teacher, "It's over. I'm not talking to you any more. Don't ask me anything. I'll ignore the marks you give me, even if they're the worst. I'll compensate for it in my other subjects." Then I went to all the other teachers, and I told the arts teacher, "I'm good. You have to give me a 1." The best grade is a 1. And I went to the other teachers and negotiated my marks, except for the core subjects for which I couldn't. I ended up having to take the tests in math, physics, German, and English. But I negotiated the other grades. And I came out pretty well.

Role models in sports and politics

MORROW Who was your sports hero when you were a young man?

PLATTNER Jesse Owens, because he won in the four classic disciplines of field and track. At that time, nobody really supported and promoted him. You might remember that he was not very welcome in Germany in 1936. But he was clearly the superior athlete of his generation.

MORROW What about a political hero?

PLATTNER I have personal ties to South Africa. My mother migrated to South Africa 27 years ago, and I spent two and a half years in South Africa, beginning in 1970. I've followed the history of South Africa for the last 27 years. When I was there, I spent most of my time in Cape Town, where Robin Island prison was. There was much talk about the prisoner Mandela. And now, he's president. I think the way Mandela behaved when he was released after 27 years was first-class, the actions of a professional politician.

I saw Robin Island and I heard the stories from the other side. I have a golf course in South Africa—a hotel and golf estate in George—and just last week, we got a visitor from the parliament. He is 71 years old and plays golf with an 11 handicap. But he didn't play golf for 40 years because he was in prison for 26 years. He is one of Mandela's friends. To be a part of history and to be able to see, touch, and talk to these people is really an unusual experience. I think the fact that they made it without major turmoil is an achievement. And they are very proud of it.

MORROW Now I understand much more about your naming your boat "Morning Glory."

PLATTNER Yes. The morning glory is a creeper and a very popular flower in Cape Town. The area where I have a home is full of morning glories.

MORROW You obviously love teaching. You teach young people. You've been honored with an honorary doctorate and professorship. Why, given your intellectual achievement, did you choose to go to IBM, rather than stay in the university and become an academic?

University—a disappointed love affair

PLATTNER I struggled with that decision for quite a while. I started in Karlsruhe, and we had a very famous professor—famous for Germany—Professor Steinbuch, who worked for Standard Electric Lawrence. He was the first in Germany to build a professional computer with transistors. That was how I came to study digital systems.

I gave three students lessons to help improve their scores. They all scored A, and I scored B minus because I had an argument with Professor Steinbuch about the test. He asked me, "What would happen if a ferrite core became smaller and smaller and smaller? What would happen to the hysteresis?" I said, "It would get smaller and smaller." He wanted to hear that it would get sharper edges, and I disagreed. So I got a B minus. That was my institute of choice, and I had wanted to become an assistant there and work on my thesis. I was so disappointed that I left the university immediately and did not go back at all to Karlsruhe for 10 years. I joined IBM. I still had some work to finish at school, but I joined IBM at the age of 24, which was unusual. I think that was the right move. I always had an advantage, being much younger than all my other colleagues.

Morrow Tell me about your first job at IBM and your
impressions of the IBM culture at that time.

Plattner I had an appointment in Böblingen in the
research lab. Unfortunately, the person I wanted to
meet, the lab manager, was in Poughkepsie and not
available. So IBM referred me to an event in Stuttgart
where they only recruited people for the field. And
somebody there told me, "Oh, no. In the lab, they lie
around on their sofas and they just relax and think. No,
the real action is in the field. You have to come to the
field." I don't know why, but this guy convinced me to
go to the field, and I joined IBM in the field.

So university was over, and science was over for me. I
became a consultant (in modern terms) for hardware
and software at IBM.

Morrow Legend has it that in IBM in those days, people
in the field were told, "This isn't necessarily the best
computer in the world, but it is the most expensive. Go
sell it."

Plattner In Karlsruhe, we had the second-fastest Control
Data computer. In my last year there, at nighttime, I
was working on a 1 million instructions-per-second
computer. Then I went to IBM, and the field had computers of 30,000 instructions per second. It was difficult
to get adjusted to this commercial world but very good
for the education.

IBM's strength was its achievements at the customer
site. Clearly in those days, IBM was customer-focused.
That was before IBM was forced to charge for services.
We were taught, and we lived up to the idea, that we
had to serve customers and do our best. If we did the
best for them, it would help them in their jobs and they
would buy more computers.

Morrow How did being raised and educated in Europe and being European—and being German, especially—shape your view of information technology? How did it make your perspective different from that of American leaders such as Larry Ellison or Scott McNealy?

The European heritage— diversity

Plattner Within IBM, we were very "local" in the sense that we were in IBM Germany and IBM Europe, and IBM USA was so far away. But when we left IBM and started SAP, our first customer was Imperial Chemical Industries (ICI), a multinational company. Starting the first day, I had to speak in English 25 percent of the time because any serious manager at ICI was English— or not German, at least. The first presentation I gave at ICI was in English. It helped us to accelerate from 0 to 50 on a scale of 100 toward international business. I think it was very important for SAP that ICI was a multinational company, which broadened our view immediately.

The first customer and first "development center" of SAP: ICI (Imperial Chemical Industries) in Östringen.

Right away in the first year, we learned how difficult it is that the French have totally different views and that the British have particular views about how to conduct business and how to run their computer systems. ICI had major operations in the Netherlands and its European headquarters in Brussels. So our first customer was totally international, and we got involved in all these deals and negotiations. It took many, many years until we could sell our software to the non-German parts of ICI. But I think ICI is the root of the idea of integration and international software that we pursued. We were lucky to have ICI as our first customer.

How founding
SAP came
about

MORROW How did you meet your fellow founders of SAP, and what was your early relationship with them?

PLATTNER We all worked at the IBM local office in Mannheim. I sat face-to-face with Dietmar Hopp, and we did the first real-time order processing system for ICI in our IBM times. Another colleague, Dr. Claus Wellenreuther, was writing financial software. He had written a little batch program and installed it 15 times, and he wanted IBM to adopt this software and make it a major initiative. The three of us together asked IBM whether we could do this within IBM. IBM said, "No, no, we have labs to do this development. Go sell computers. Or go help install computers. Other people will take care of software development." And we were not allowed to do it. Actually, I'm not so sure SAP would allow people sitting in an office in Marseilles to develop a new version of the SAP system!

So we decided to leave IBM. Two other colleagues, Klaus Tschira and Hans-Werner Hector, joined us, so we started as five people with three employees. Tschira brought the operating-system knowledge. We were all DOS people, and he had the most operating-system experience. He was serving the large implementations here.

At that time, people were leaving IBM to start consulting companies. But we left with the sole goal of developing standard software. That was our number-one goal, and we kept that goal the focus of all our subsequent undertaking. That was very important. Despite the fact that our first project was a custom software development, we only had standard software in mind. And only 18 months after we started in 1972, we released our first standard software.

In the beginning, we were all programmers. All five of us wrote programs. And we all consulted, and we all sold software. Perhaps that's totally different from some US start-ups. Some of us were more successful than others in selling, but in the first three years, we did everything. Everybody worked at night, and we had to write and test the software at night. We had to consult in daytime, and we had to travel to sell the product.

MORROW Was this the legendary R/1?

PLATTNER This was R/1. We called it "System R." We didn't know in those days that there would be an R/2 and an R/3. I remember in the second year, when we were traveling in Switzerland, Claus Wellenreuther said, "We might achieve perhaps 100 to 200 installations." I said, "Wow, that's a large number," knowing that we were struggling to get customer number six. System R achieved between 70 and 80 installations by the end of the 1970s.

MORROW I gather that in the first year, you nearly doubled the size of your staff from five to nine employees.

Careful growth and well thought-out expenditures

PLATTNER In the first year, we essentially doubled our staff to around 10 employees. And we were growing pretty slowly—not as aggressively as the young start-ups in the Bay Area. But we had a great time in the mid-1970s. We had years in which we had 50 percent profit before tax.

Perhaps interesting from an entrepreneurial point of view is the fact that we self-financed the whole company during the first 15 years. We never went to a bank and asked for money; we always financed ourselves. We were the sole owners when we decided to go public.

MORROW You never had to tap into the venture capital community?

PLATTNER Never. I'm not against venture capital. I think it is a great infrastructure in the United States because it really accelerated the rebound of the economy in the 1990s, especially in the high-tech industry. When I thought the high-tech industry was lost to Japan, all of a sudden, semiconductor technology and software were back. We didn't do it this way in Germany; we made it by careful growth and wise spending. We still had enough money to buy perhaps not the fanciest cars, but good cars.

The first quotation of SAP shares on the Frankfurt stock exchange (October 1988).

Before beginning to develop R/2, we got another international customer, John Deere, in Mannheim. John
Deere came up with the idea that our software should
run on one computer and serve several countries—or
rather, several legal entities with different legislation
and different languages. John Deere had the world
divided I think into Division I, which was the Americas,
and Division II, which was Europe and Africa. So the
languages needed were German, French, and English,
at a minimum.

In 1975 and 1976, we changed the system from a
one-language-only system to a multilingual system.
One of our hallmarks later was that instead of having
different versions of the system, one computer system
could serve users in France, South Africa, Germany,
and England.

MORROW So it was being close to the customer that drove
the innovation.

PLATTNER Being close to customers has always helped to
drive our innovation.

John Deere asked us to internationalize the software,
and we did. It was the beginning of our international
version of SAP Systems. That was a big step in those
days. Then, we got more customers, and we got
Freudenberg and Grundig Television Systems. They
were large IMS customers.

The integration of IMS was painful. We had three installations of that type, and they were very expensive for
us to support. It was a starting point for the development of the next-generation software in 1979. That's
when we moved to Walldorf, and we had about 80
people. Most of them were developers. In those days,
we didn't hire consultants. We hired developers, and
they had to do the same work as we did as much as
possible. That means they had to design, code, test,
sell, and consult.

MORROW And you had a funny story to tell?

PLATTNER In 1973, we had one of the most critical situations in our 25-year history. It was very early in the development of our standard software product (not the first version we installed at ICI). In those days, our programs were on punched cards. The punched cards were in iron boxes—2,000 punched cards in each box. We had to carry the punched cards from one computer to the other. One day, I took the metal box out of my car. It was a rainy day as usual in Germany, and as I walked through the parking lot, I stumbled and dropped the box. All 2,000 punched cards of one of the core portions of our system scattered on the ground.

MORROW Oh, no. What did you do?

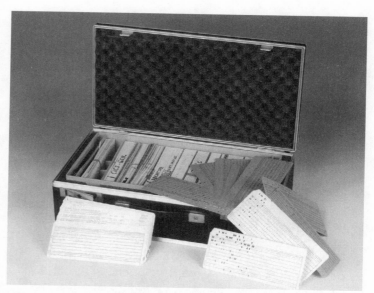

Boxes with punched cards (System R).

PLATTNER It took me two days to reconstruct it all. It's a standard joke in SAP about how dangerous it is for me to carry cards. The company could have been dead.

MORROW Why did you move to Walldorf, of all the places in Germany?

Moving to Walldorf

PLATTNER Actually, that was not my favorite decision. We had another alternative to go to Schwetzingen, which is close to Heidelberg. I preferred that one. In those days, we still had our headquarters in Weinheim, which is a nice town north of Heidelberg, and I lived there, as did Wellenreuther and Hector; so three of the five lived there. But my partner, Dietmar Hopp, lived in Walldorf.

Dietmar and Klaus went to the mayor in Weinheim, who told them, "No. We have Freudenberg, and we have another big company, Naturin. We don't need another company, so I can't give you any special terms." Walldorf had no industry in those days—just little construction companies and some repair shops. So Walldorf was keen and offered us a huge property for very little money. We couldn't beat that. So I had to drive, and Dietmar Hopp had the short five-minute drive from his home.

MORROW How many employees were there when you first came to Walldorf?

PLATTNER I think we had about 80 employees when we first came to Walldorf. But they were not all based here. Most of them were stationed at a customer site. In our headquarters in Walldorf, we had perhaps 10 permanent employees, not more.

Soon after that, in 1980, we got our first computer here, a Siemens computer, which was a real milestone in our history. It was over on the other side of this building.

MORROW I heard also that by 1986, the largest capital investment you had made, besides the building, was an IBM mainframe that you bought.

PLATTNER Yes. It's unusual for software companies to do this, but we paid for all the buildings. And we built them. When we made some money in the late 1970s and the early 1980s, we built our own buildings; we didn't rent buildings anymore. We owned everything that we used for the production of our software. Next, we bought computers. We got an IBM mainframe. From then on, we grew bigger and bigger, and the friendship with IBM improved. Then we became a large IBM customer.

The R/2 system

This brings us to the days of R/2, which started in the early 1980s. We started the development in 1979, as I said, when we struggled with the final phase of our System R. The R/2 system at its peak had 2,200 implementations.

The first company building of its own on Max Planck Street in the industrial district of Walldorf (1980).

I should point out that we're still developing R/2. We still have 200 people in the development and maintenance of the software because we still have 2,000 installations worldwide. We're providing the changes for the euro, we're developing two new IBM mainframe releases for the system, and we'll celebrate the 20th anniversary in the R/2 development team pretty soon. Some of the software that Dietmar, Claus, and I wrote is still in use.

(Editor's note: At the end of 1999, about 100 developers were still taking care of 850 R/2 installations worldwide. In the meantime, more than 95 percent of the old R/2 customers have migrated over to R/3.)

MORROW Did you work on financial applications?

The SAP board of directors in the spring of 1988, with the founders (from left to right)) Klaus E. Tschira, Hasso Plattner, Dietmar Hopp, and Hans-Werner Hector.

PLATTNER I did everything—technology, financial applications, some interpreters, and the dialogue part of the system. But yes, for 17 years, I was responsible for the financial applications. I wrote a significant amount of code.

I got into that just by chance. When we started to develop our first standard system, we had to split up our efforts. I wanted to do the sales part of the system, and Dietmar said, "I'll do purchasing." Claus said, "I'll do financials." But as it happened, we couldn't sell sales and distribution systems; in those days, you couldn't standardize the sales and distribution system of a company. So I concentrated on financials and the purchasing part, and Claus Wellenreuther continued with a small system. We had the System R part of the company, and we had the little System F. System F existed until the end of the 1970s, and then in 1980, Claus Wellenreuther left SAP. That happened one afternoon, and then I had to learn financials, and that's how it started. But I still did some parts of the technology. Especially in the R/2 system, I did more technology than applications.

Underway toward a client/server architecture

MORROW You are credited with being among the principal leaders who moved SAP from mainframe applications to client/server architecture.

PLATTNER Yes. In the late 1980s, IBM announced systems application architecture (SAA). That day, or the next day, we started the project to develop our third generation of software. The equation was pretty simple. IBM said, "The programming language is C, and it's cooperative processing." We used Presentation Manager as the front end and SQL as the database. So basically, there was a well-defined set of ingredients and infrastructure, and we started the project. I collected a bunch of people and got rid of all my other duties and started the R/3 project.

The period from 1988 until 1992 was a wonderful time. I didn't travel at all. I just sat here in the lab and developed. I had meetings every day and walked around. I enjoyed that. It was a great time. I knew this development would not be allowed to fail.

Then we learned in the early 1990s that IBM wouldn't make it—that SAA was perhaps a trap. That was another critical point in SAP's history. This is how it really happened. It's not that we were so bright and thought about it and had this great strategy.

In around 1988, we had already decided to develop the foundation of the new software on UNIX computers. We did this silently. We had all the ingredients— SQL, C, and distributed computing—on UNIX computers. OS/2 was still not running, and there was no way to run UNIX on mainframes. So we developed all the infrastructure software, including our fourth-generation language, ABAP/4. This involved redeveloping this language and re-implementing everything in C running on UNIX. Then, we were able to develop the new application on a DB2-based mainframe using our ABAP/4 language. The application developers didn't know that the system was not running on UNIX computers—that it was running on an old mainframe.

I think it was a clever idea. And then we wanted to marry the two systems and bring the C-code-based system together with the ABAP/4-based application. That happened in late 1990 or early 1991. And we were struggling. And the reason was very, very funny.

C was running on a mainframe. So we got our C-based system converted to the mainframe because that was the number-one goal: for SAA, the IBM system, to be portable. IBM didn't think about UNIX, but they thought of OS/2, and OS/2 was much closer to UNIX than anything else.

Going to the
Hannover Fair

The system ran under IMS, but we couldn't debug it. On our super-large mainframe in those days, a four-processor mainframe, the first program I requested was a debugger. So I put together a UNIX developer, responsible for the C code, and a seasoned IBM mainframe developer and told them to start debugging. They switched on Time Sharing Option (TSO) to start a debugger, and guess what happened? One of the four processors stalled.

Then the second programmer ran into a problem and switched on the debugger. Two processors went down. Our CFO complained, "Our terminals are not working. What's going on? Something is wrong." Our 200 R/2 developers complained, "Well, this is a bad day today. I think we'd better knock off and go home."

Then, the third and the fourth R/3 developers switched on the debugger because they all had to debug. We were aiming to go to the Hannover Fair in six weeks and unveil the system for the first time. This fair was our big, big, big target.

All four processors were dead. Peter Zencke said, "Perhaps we should try to migrate the application from the mainframe down to this workstation. Perhaps it will work, because it worked the other way. Why shouldn't it work?"

MORROW And it freed up the four processors?

PLATTNER And we were ready for the Hannover Fair with this little computer, a single workstation. I said, "But this is not what we want to sell." "I totally agree with you," he said, "But we can make the Hannover Fair." I said, "Okay, do what you want. I'm going home now. It's late. Give it a try."

R/3 is a UNIX system

Fifteen people—actually, fourteen people, because I was leaving the room—jumped on this workstation, and everybody opened a window. We had only one keyboard. They were working simultaneously. I have never seen people more eager to succeed. They immediately started to migrate the software down to the workstation, we made the Hannover Fair, and there was the new system. We were running on a UNIX workstation. And we couldn't hide it anymore that we developed everything on UNIX.

So basically, they lured it out of us that R/3 is a UNIX system. Yet the image remains that R/3 originally was a mainframe system. But it never ran on a mainframe.

The next day, I got an invitation from HP, asking us to look at its workstations. HP had a prototype workstation twice as fast as the Digital workstation. I said, "I am so impressed. Twice the speed and more to come." I instantly bought 200 workstations. HP said, "It's impossible to fulfill your order." I said, "Okay. We're an IBM shop. Our second supplier is Digital. If you want to have a deal with SAP, jump." And within six weeks, we got 200 workstations. We installed them here in our other development center, and we had 50 times the computing power of our large mainframe—50 times the computing power!

Within another six weeks, we solved the distributed computing problem. This is when we invented three-tier client/server architecture. How do we exploit the computing power of 200 computers? And synchronize a central repository? That is what R/3 is all about—a centralized repository with distributed computing power. And from the first day that these machines started running, and Hewlett-Packard helped us to get this distribution done, we had a totally different system.

The day R/3 was born

We had no shortage in computing power. Every single developer had a machine nearly twice as fast as one of our mainframes, or at least as fast as one of our mainframe processors, for himself. So the testing continued. Our development speed leapfrogged, and that was a breakthrough for R/3. Actually, that was the day R/3 was born.

So R/3 really owes its birth to the necessity of getting to the Hannover Fair. This is the true story.

In summary, Imperial Chemicals was the perfect first customer. John Deere was the perfect customer for internationalization. Then we ran into a crisis and had to get to the Hannover Fair, we were forced by necessity to use the HP 9000, and R/3 emerged. Suddenly, we were running on workstations.

The first R/3 customers

MORROW Was there a pivotal first customer for R/3?

PLATTNER Yes. The idea of R/3 was to build a system for the AS/400. AS/400s were small computers, and we wanted to cover the low end of the market because R/2 was well-established on the high end and we had no intention of shutting down R/2. So R/3 was meant to cover the low end of the market. Now, we couldn't run on the AS/400; it didn't physically work. C was not there, and in those days the ingredients of SAA hadn't arrived on the AS/400. It was obvious that SAA was going to collapse. The Whitewater financial applications project collapsed in IBM, and the advanced manufacturing project in Atlanta was shut down. With 2,000 people working on a manufacturing system, this situation was our biggest threat ever. And OfficeVision was struggling and later abandoned. We said, "Now we have to move on to UNIX and go for the low end of the market."

Despite the fact that we had nearly unlimited computing power, we were limited by the capacity of the database. The first prospect in Germany for R/3 was a supposedly "medium-sized" market company dealing with screws, a large screw dealer. The company had $2 billion in revenues in 1991 and was operating in 80 countries in the world. Suddenly, we realized that this "middle-market" customer had one of the largest warehouses in Germany and was—as far as transaction rate is concerned—larger than the largest R/2 customer in operation. That meant from day one, all our ideas about how to address the low end of the market got stalled.

MORROW Who discovered this screw manufacturer?

The clever sales representative

PLATTNER A sales rep. A sales rep found out that this company was very modern. The company said, "We will not install a mainframe product. We will go to UNIX." And the sales rep was clever enough to think, "Aren't we working on a UNIX system here?" So our first R/3 customer in Germany was a large company operating internationally, and there we were again.

The first production R/3 customer was a very small company in Denmark, called Kemira, a subsidiary of a Finnish company. We had a fantastic relationship for a remote implementation, and we did this implementation because our R/2 implementation there had been painful. Kemira was a UNIX company, and we had implemented R/2 in its computer center, and the company was not happy. So I had made the promise, "As soon as we have a UNIX system, we'll replace your system." So Kemira was our first production customer in mid-1992. And then we reached the climax of the fun stories.

MORROW It's just a perfect chronology of incredibly fortunate events.

PLATTNER Yes.

MORROW Being close to the customer seems to be the key element in that success.

The key to success

PLATTNER Being close to the customer is the key element. It's also key either to understand intellectually or just to feel that something is going on—something is going to change—and to be ready for the change. Perhaps

The board of directors council (1988).

you don't have to be the forerunner. But if you see the crowds starting to run, you'd better be in the first third.

MORROW R/3 has, of course, taken the world by storm. You said that there was a great story about getting into the United States.

R/3 in America

PLATTNER In 1992, SAP was a seasoned company that had been in operation for 20 years, and we had spent millions and millions on the development of R/3. We planned the rollout of R/3 like a military operation. We had planned for 200 implementations in Germany and in English-speaking Europe for the second half of 1992. Our first R/3 customers were small companies, which was our intention. R/2 was occupying the high end of the market, and we wanted small companies for R/3. So we weren't making much money with the R/3 system.

Then, as you remember, 1992 was the year of the downturn of the IBM mainframe. All of a sudden, mainframe sales stalled.

MORROW End of the world.

PLATTNER End of the world. And you know where all our competitors from 1992 are today! It was two weeks before the SAP user meeting in Orlando, SAPPHIRE 1992. I met with Dietmar Hopp, and he said, "What can we do?" I said, "We could start selling R/3 in the United States." And he said, "Okay. Let's do it."

But the system was not ready. The system would be ready, and it was committed to be ready at the beginning of 1993, in three months. So we said, "We'll announce that the system will be ready three months from now and that we will ship it early next year."

I went to Orlando. I had already spent a lot of time in the United States, and I knew how the analysts and the press think. There I was onstage, with an R/3 system under a cover in a UNIX box, ready to be unveiled. Close to the end of the speech, I said, "We're having great success with R/3 in Europe. We've already installed 100 systems." That was true. And I said, "We're ahead of schedule. Whoever orders R/3 today at this user conference will get shipment within six weeks. I guarantee it. And whoever detects a flaw in the English translation in the system will get the software replaced or updated within six weeks, or we will provide a translator on-site."

When you deliver a speech, you know whether or not you're in tune with your audience. There was applause. The press went wild. We got the first customer two weeks after that, Convex Computers in Dallas.

I flew from Orlando to Los Angeles. I saw all the small manufacturing companies in Los Angeles, and I said, "These should be our customers. I want to have the small ones." But the first prospect we ran into was Chevron Oil.

MORROW Some small company!

PLATTNER Some small company! We worked for six weeks. We flew Chevron over to this little Kemira company in Denmark. There was big Chevron with Kemira, the fertilizer producer. Chevron was both an upstream and downstream oil company—number 10 in the United States.

We won. We won against Oracle, and we won against J.D. Edwards, SSA, and all the others because Chevron wanted a UNIX system. That meant that R/3 was suddenly in the big league on top of R/2. We had to change all our development plans. We couldn't stop it anymore. A gold rush started. We were lucky again.

We had the right product, a UNIX-based product, when the entire world was about to downsize. Downsizing was the number-one buzzword in 1992 and early 1993, and we had a product. It wasn't perfect—by far not as perfect as the R/2 system. But everybody had seen the functionality that SAP could deliver and they trusted us.

So that was the history of the transition from R/3 being a system for the small AS/400 market to being on top of R/2 with the biggest players in the United States, with global implementations.

MORROW Fantastic. All this coincided, of course, with the reengineering revolution and the downsizing revolution in the United States.

Tell me about your vision of partnership. I've heard that one of the reasons for your success is that you're one of the easiest companies in the world to partner with and that you're a very good partner—that you don't compete with your partners.

PLATTNER Opinions differ on that. Sometimes we are diffi-cult, and sometimes we are easy. There was no ques-tion when the explosion of demand for support started that we had to team up. We had always planned to team up with the hardware vendors. And there was no question that in the United States, we would work with the established service and consulting industry in the IT business, which is the Big Six. And we knew the Big Six already, and they had occasionally helped us in some implementations. We had an ongoing relationship with Andersen Consulting for many years, actually; for some time, we had a joint venture in Germany for the low end of the market. And so it was just natural to talk to them, and we pursued it aggressively.

We always wanted to remain a software-development company. We did not want to become too consulting-oriented and end up being a consulting company that couldn't afford to do software development. That was our biggest fear. So it was natural to partner with the Big Six. And it was not to increase sales; it was because they could do the implementation or help to restructure and reorganize a company. And it was to promote the idea of integrated software.

The idea: integrated software

Even in the 1990s, integrated software was a new idea in the United States. It was also new to the rest of the world, although it was known in Germany from the mid-1970s. We had established the term "integrated applications software," and it was actually hard to sell non-integrated applications software in Germany, whether SAP's or other competitors' software. But America still had separate software components with a batch interface. Even today, our competitors think that's the better way. But finally today, in the late 1990s, integrated systems are the new world. SAP brought integrated applications to the market, and the Big Six helped us to promote the idea and manage expectations in large companies.

MORROW One of the other things that is most impressive about SAP is not only the depth of the use of applications, but the breadth—the number of different kinds of businesses that can use the software. You didn't go into the United States as an absolute newcomer. There were 50 implementations of R/2 there.

Internation-
alization

PLATTNER Yes. We started in the mid-1980s to internationalize. We founded our international headquarters in Switzerland, and we were quite successful in exporting R/2 to the world. It was in about 1986 that DuPont, Mobil Oil, and Dow Chemical in America started to look into Europe and say, "What's going on in Europe? What kind of software are you using there? How can you integrate—in the case of DuPont—10 countries on one computer sitting in Frankfurt? You run the financials for France, Italy, Spain, England, the Netherlands, and Germany on one computer. How can this happen?" And the countries explained to their American headquarters that they were using SAP software.

We had a software congress here in Germany, and 25 people from Mobil came over. I asked them, "Are you going to buy SAP software? You'll never buy SAP software. You'll go with MSA. Or you'll go with McCormick and Dodge. You will never buy. You're not serious." They said, "Do you want to make a bet?" And I said, "Yes." Three months later, they bought SAP software. This is how we actually entered the market.

We opened an office in Philadelphia to be close to the oil and chemical industry, specifically DuPont and Mobil. Dow was a little bit further away. That's how it started. We already had offices in Philadelphia and in Chicago. We opened an office in the R/2 days in California—a very small office in Redwood Shores, just a few yards away from Oracle. And we got only very large multinational companies who adopted the idea of integrated application software—with the software reconciling data internally and the data being consistent among accounting, financial accounting, cost accounting, and manufacturing.

There were limitations. None of the published charts indicated that there was some invasion of the market by a German company! We were the "weird guys" competing with Walker Interactive in some arenas, but not mainstream.

MORROW Your R/2 beachhead was nonthreatening because it was mainframe-based.

PLATTNER Yes, it was nonthreatening. We were good, and we were a niche player. And we had some infrastructure there: We knew the people, and we especially knew the Big Six such as Andersen and Price Waterhouse. Then R/3 arrived, and we were doing two things. Our US president in those days, Klaus Besier, sensed immediately that this was dynamite.

After the SAPPHIRE in Orlando in 1992, we saw the first interest in UNIX systems as complementary to the big mainframe software.

German technology and American marketing

I wanted to change the compensation for our sales team in California. Until then, SAP was an engineering company, like Digital, and the salespeople had salaries. The Americans told me, "In California, that's not possible. We have to be on commission. We want to run the risk." So we introduced commissions in California. That was a big deal in Walldorf. Nobody in Walldorf wanted it. I said, "We'll just do a little experiment in California." I flew back to Germany, and I had not even landed in Frankfurt when I started hearing already about what had happened in the United States. "They have commissions everywhere. Salespeople are on commission! Are you crazy?"

The market was ripe, and the product was ready. We got a bunch of salespeople immediately because they could make a fortune. This is the United States. It's totally different. The salespeople didn't live and die for SAP. They wanted to make a fortune. They saw the product, they saw the opportunity, and they came. They left Oracle, they left the other competitors, and all of a sudden, we had one of the strongest sales teams in the world. It is an American story as much as a European story.

So the European engineers, with our stubbornness in solving detailed problems, worked on things silently in the lab—not talking about them and not announcing the product before drawing the first sketches of the system. We worked on the system, and then we announced it. We delivered it immediately. That part was totally different from the American way. But we sold it in the American style.

MORROW American salesmen, German engineering. What could be better? There is a legend that a German engineer ported R/3 to Windows NT in five days. Is it true?

R/3 on Windows NT

PLATTNER This is true. You might hear many stories from our competitors and others that R/3 is a copy of the R/2 system and that we just migrated it. But we really redeveloped everything. As we discussed earlier, we had struggled with the IBM SAA platform, and we developed the system on two completely different computer systems. So we had a highly portable system.

Windows NT is different from UNIX, but not too far off. When Microsoft came up with Windows NT, one of the five key people who developed the kernel of the system said, "I want to try it." And he got a Windows NT system, and he took all the interfaces and replaced them. We have 50 operating-system interfaces. When he replaced 10 of them, the system started running immediately. After five days, he was able to demonstrate a complete transaction running on Windows NT. That gave us some impetus!

You won't believe this, but our Windows NT development group is still very small. I think it has fewer than four people. The rest of the development still happens in UNIX. We were the first major UNIX software provider or distributed client/server software provider who could jump on Windows NT. At least one fourth of our installations are now on Windows NT.

MORROW You were international from the time of your very first big customer, Imperial Chemical. R/3 is, of course, the success story in global computing. There has been a succession of new eras, and we're entering into another one, the Internet. Who had heard of the Internet three years ago, except as the system that academics and universities use? As someone who has seen this industry change the world, are you as excited about the potential for the future as you have been about the past in solving these problems?

PLATTNER Remember what my art teacher told me? When we developed the R/3 system here, we had an employee from California, and he had these weird ideas. He wanted to bring his bike in and keep it in the office. I said, "That's impossible. We can't keep a bike in the office." And I asked, "Why?" He said, "It's raining outside." It seemed totally strange to us to keep a bike in your office. Well, they do it at Apple and at other companies in Silicon Valley. And this guy always told me, "Watch the Internet. Watch the Internet. Something's coming." This was in 1991.

He left SAP to travel the world. He told me that perhaps he would join SAP again later, somewhere in the world. I haven't met him again. But when he left, he wrote me a long letter. "Don't forget the Internet, please. I fear that when I leave, nobody will take care of the Internet. Nobody understands what is coming here." I kept this letter.

I didn't see the Internet coming. I just didn't see it. And all of a sudden, it was there. All of a sudden, people started talking about the Internet. And you know how

"Watch the Internet"

enthused people can get in the United States! Then the venture capitalists got involved, and everything started bubbling up in 1995. And there was the Internet. "We will change everything." I thought, "What is it? Just to jump from one page to another page to another page? Is this all you have?" Then I remembered what the guy had said—"Watch it. Watch it." And we were aware of the Internet. We talked about it. We just couldn't use it when it first bubbled up in 1995.

By last year, everybody was asking us, "What are you doing with the Internet? What is your vision of the Internet?" And our standard answer was, "What is *your* vision?" because we are always driven by our customers' needs. In the past, they had asked us for more applications, and for more functionality, and to go into new industries. This time, the companies came to us and asked, "What are you doing with the Internet?"

Early last year, we really started development. We said, "Obviously, we have to be a player in the Internet." We talked to Microsoft. Microsoft was in the same situation: "What should we do with the Internet?" We talked a lot with Microsoft. The first outcome of the discussions was that we went to the Hannover Fair together and announced that we had developed the Business APIs. Business APIs are our contribution to the Internet. They enable people on the Internet anywhere to access SAP systems and work with SAP systems interactively.

On the stage
with Bill Gates

After we announced the BAPIs in Vienna, we demonstrated them in Philadelphia, where I had perhaps one of my best days in marketing. I convinced Bill Gates to come onstage and do a two-hour session with me. We practiced the day before, and I think it was one of the best presentations each of us ever gave. It was great entertainment for the audience. We actually worked live on our SAP and Microsoft integrated Internet system. For an hour and a half, we demonstrated software that had never been demonstrated before.

MORROW You and Bill Gates?

PLATTNER Yes.

MORROW Onstage together?

PLATTNER We did it! And we had no problems. We circumvented all the little buggy parts of the system. He had a system breakdown in a PowerPoint slide show, though.

That was the marketing breakthrough for our Internet solution. Today, we are a major commercial player in the Internet. We build Internet solutions. Actual production solutions with heavy-duty administration and an integrated sales system are still rare, but we team up with Intel or Microsoft and with other players in the industry.

Back to the future

Hasso Plattner and Bill Gates at a joint presentation at SAPPHIRE in Philadelphia 1996.

All our documentation, all our training material, and everything we know are on an Internet server called SAPNet now. We just shipped or installed it four days ago, and it's working. All the information we have is now available on the Internet if you have access rights to all the security levels. Nothing is hidden. As long as you are a partner, a development partner, a consulting partner, or a customer, you can access this information.

We can already see how the Internet will change the way we do business. Many human brokers will be replaced by electronic brokers. Application brokerage is the future of reservation systems, airline systems, rent-a-car systems, product catalogs—you name it. The ideas and concepts of three years ago are becoming reality today. Three years from now, the way people and companies deal with each other will have changed substantially.

Some people said, "It's too late for SAP. SAP will get hammered. This old-fashioned R/2 system that just migrated to the client/server world can't make it to the Internet." But it made it. How did we achieve it? Perhaps we put more engineering in the system than any American competitor ever thought.

MORROW Pure brainpower.

The German way: be perfect, not just shiny

PLATTNER Perhaps it's this crazy German attitude to make it perfect—to be to some extent perfect, not only to be "shiny." We learned our marketing lessons, and we always have been, from a German perspective, kind of showmen. But we have a decent technology behind us. And that is, I think, what enabled us over the years to take the technology onslaughts again and again and react to them—sometimes within a few weeks, sometimes a little bit later.

We nearly missed the PC because we thought the PC was a toy. We were totally protected by the mainframe world, sitting in a mainframe glass house, and we didn't take the PC seriously. And that did harm to us. All of a sudden, a company like Lotus and companies like Borland and Microsoft were bigger than SAP. We couldn't believe it. We thought, "How can you make so much money with a spreadsheet or a word processor? We have complete applications." We thought we had the applications, but years later, these others called themselves the applications companies.

MORROW An SAP employee who is in charge of R/2 services was quoted as saying that one of the things that makes SAP a great company is that it is a non-bureaucratic community of intelligent people.

Organization: find the right size

PLATTNER That's true. It has made us successful, and yet we still struggle with it.

MORROW Is it hard to be nonbureaucratic?

PLATTNER It's perhaps easy to be nonbureaucratic, but it's difficult to achieve all that we have achieved by being nonbureaucratic on the one hand and precise on the other hand. That's a very complex thing. I don't believe

The SAP Research and Development Center in Palo Alto, California.

that we could have done much better with a more regulated internal structure. On the other hand, we need
internal structures, and sometimes we struggle because
suddenly, it starts hurting.

We have pretty much relied on the flexibility of our
people. They have done the best they could, and it is
very, very important to us that we have become a truly
global company and that we have development in
America and in Japan.

SAP has a very well-organized worldwide sales and
consulting organization, and we still maintain as much
flexibility in our development labs as we need to
remain creative. If you establish very well-organized
structures, many people will have excuses. As long as
you are more flexible in your organization, you can
blame more people for not seeing what was about to
come or for seeing it too late.

Japan—a
challenge

MORROW Tell me about Japan.

PLATTNER As usual, we did it for customers. This time, the
German chemical multinationals asked us to go to
Japan. Then DuPont joined them in asking. So we got
pressure from the United States and from Germany to
export our software to Japan. Because SAP was known
for precision engineering, they wanted to have a full-
blown Japanese version, meaning everything had to
be in Japanese. They told us from day one, "It's great
to have an English system. But you won't sell it in
Japan. And you'll only make it if you sell it to Japanese
companies."

MORROW How big a challenge was that?

PLATTNER That was a big challenge. It was a humongous
challenge. It was the largest investment we ever made
in a single task or single objective. We invested for
three years to build a full-blown, two-digit, double-byte
character version of the system, and every single word

is in Japanese. All documentation, all screens—
everything. All the people working in the office in
Japan are Japanese. Americans and Germans only sit
in a back office.

We were rich enough to afford to do this, and we did
it. Today, Japan is our third-largest market. Our largest
markets are the United States, then Germany, then
Japan. It was worth the investment.

MORROW What was the most agonizing part of that
process?

PLATTNER When you look at the Japanese screen, it is
worse than any other language because you cannot
read it; you can't see anything. So we did all the testing in German or English. Then the Japanese system
had to work inside the system flawlessly. We hired
Japanese people for translation, and we hired Japanese people to retest the system. It is a single system,
and the only system in the world currently, that can run
both Japanese and English in a single system. It's a
technical miracle.

And it was a big selling point to all high-tech companies on the West Coast because they have ties into
Japan. All of a sudden, we got the HPs, the Apples,
and the Digitals sitting on the East Coast and Compaq
Computers, Intel, and, finally, Microsoft.

We expanded the internal system to handle double
bytes. Now that the system is fully flexible to handle
double bytes, one system not only handles Japanese,
but also Chinese, Korean, and all the other languages
that require a double-byte system.

It's still work to do this. But this flexibility was a selling
point. It's multicurrency. That's the biggest advantage
for a European company. We support the many currencies. And now, we're getting another currency, the euro,
on top and parallel. No one in America understands

that we are dealing with two currencies here in each country. And we have different currencies in each country. That's a complexity that American software doesn't handle well. We also have different tax laws in each state of the European Union. We have the authorities in Brussels, but we have different tax laws, and variations, and they are much greater than the variations you know in the United States. So our system is multicurrency, multilegal, and multilingual.

The SAP concepts are right up to data

In one system, we have to speak several languages. It is mandatory in Canada, and it is mandatory in Switzerland. It's now mandatory, basically, in every non-English-speaking state in the world because English is the language of the Internet. So you have to run your systems in two languages—in the Internet international language and your local language. Now the SAP system, by definition, runs in multiple languages. One installation can support many languages. We can install a system that is responsible for the Pacific Rim and run Australia, Japan, and mainland China in one system.

MORROW Excellent.

PLATTNER To some extent, this grew out of our European heritage. But now, with the Internet, everybody faces it. Everybody knows now it's integration. Everybody knows now it's multitiered client/server architecture. Look at the Internet with proxy servers and so on. Everybody knows now that we have to transform from one language to another language and that multilingual systems are the standard. We will never change the French, and we will never get the Japanese to give up their language. We will never get the Germans to give up their language, despite the fact that it is much closer to English than these other two languages.

Influences back and forth: SAP and its customers

MORROW One of the secrets of your success has been being close to customers, listening to their needs, and designing solutions for their problems. Do you now see companies molding their operations to fit your vision of how companies should operate most efficiently, rather than having you design something custom for them?

PLATTNER Very early we began changing the way companies did business. We've changed how companies do accounting in Germany. We changed some principles of accounting.

MORROW Can you give me some examples?

PLATTNER We didn't close books with the SAP system because we were fans of real-time information. So every little voucher is added to the system. It's there immediately. We can instantly write a balance sheet or a profit-and-loss statement at any time in the month.

MORROW So you have real-time financials without having to wait for the end of the month to close?

PLATTNER Real-time financials. And large companies were struggling with that. We have a lot of month-end closing. I said, "Okay, this has to become a real-time transaction." And we changed their thinking, to some extent.

Now, we could run larger jobs as transactions. We mechanized some of the month-end activities of a company, and they became official transactions. So companies converted these activities to transactions. And we integrated the accounts receivable, accounts payable, general ledger, and cost accounting into one physical system. Nobody had done this before.

There are some disadvantages in doing that. But it's a technically cleaner system. So we had a technically cleaner system that forced them to change their behavior. For example, they had to have the same chart of accounts in financials and in cost accounting. There cannot be two charts of accounts in our system.

MORROW In a world that is really becoming a global market, I suppose it is arguable that the most important global impact of this technology might be in finance and the flow of money. Would you say your financial applications have had the most profound effect on the world, as opposed to manufacturing?

The availability of real-time information

PLATTNER I think the most profound effect R/3 has had is the general availability of real-time information. Within a company, somebody is fulfilling a task. The task ends. And all information that was affected by this task is available immediately in the new form, in the updated form.

That means you can improve workflow significantly. In conventional organizations, it's a sequential process. You have to pass the work forward. Something changed, and somebody else has to react to that. Our idea from the beginning was let everybody do everything immediately. Then they basically have access to the latest information, wherever it is, and whatever they want to know. We struggled for many years with that. People debated it; they argued that it was not the right way to look at it.

The Internet has changed that now. The Internet gives direct access immediately to all information that is available. I now know where the parcel is that I sent from Washington, D.C., to Walldorf using Federal Express. I can use the computer to find out that it just landed in Frankfurt and is about to be shipped to Walldorf. You can do this today.

It is nothing other than our old idea of making every piece of information available in real time. Then you can reduce the number of agents or the number of workflow components you need in order to monitor somebody else's business. That plays so well.

It is actually an intellectual victory for us that so many of the original concepts of System R are in the R/3 system and can play a role now in the Internet. Everybody now understands that they cannot deal with store-and-forward information; information has to be close to real time.

If you have to get an airline ticket immediately, you don't want to wait 24 hours to find out that you have your reservation. We want to know instantly that we can fly, or we will take another airline or go through another airport. This is exactly what real-time integration means—and what it meant to us.

Therefore, I think we are mentally quite well-prepared for the Internet. And to the surprise of some of our competitors, we made it earlier to the Internet than they did, with real applications.

MORROW What is the most unusual application? I know that one of the Everest expeditions was recently planned using your software. Is there an application of SAP software that you are particularly proud of?

PLATTNER This is a difficult question. We have nearly 10,000 installations and 7,000 customers. Whom do I like best? I don't know. Perhaps the most flattering one was very recent—a start-up company with six Ph.D.s. They flew in to look at R/3. Their venture capitalists didn't approve it. The six Ph.D.s want to be a $100 million company in three years, and they wanted to buy R/3. It was so close. We couldn't get the hardware. They needed somebody who rents out the hardware.

And we have a very small company in Munich that manufactures bikes. It's very small, with 20 people. They run R/2. One of our best implementation consultants installed the whole financial system, along with a little bit of purchasing and sales, within two weeks. I'm proud of the little ones. The big ones can always make it; they have the stamina. They have the resources. And they have the brains to do it. The little ones are actually a better test of whether our system is ready for the market.

MORROW It's nice to know that a company the size of SAP still takes great pleasure in helping companies that are the size you were in 1972.

PLATTNER Yes, but it also serves our own interests. The little ones put the mirror in front of you and tell you exactly where you are right and where you are wrong. And there are no politics. They are straightforward. You get to talk to the owner. In San Luis Obispo, we have a customer where the owner not only made the decision and bought the software but, as the CFO, also implemented the system himself. The company has, I think, 100 employees.

We had a meeting in 1996 in Philadelphia, at our user conference, and I invited the five smallest customers that were at the user conference to meet with us. That was a very interesting meeting—to talk to the people who know, perhaps, more about the software than some of the super-large multinationals.

Last, but not least: R/3 on the AS/400

You asked me what is perhaps the most interesting customer or the company that is totally different from the other ones. It is the Sydney Zoo. We made a donation to the Sydney Zoo. IBM donated the AS/400 hardware, and we donated our software to demonstrate that R/3 was finally running on the AS/400.

After 10 years of development—9 years actually— we shipped finally on the AS/400. And the people from the Zoo were so flattered. They have to live on donations. It's not really a money-making enterprise. And the system is running fine. So we have all the

information for the chimpanzees and all the maintenance they have to do. It's all done and managed by
an R/3 system.

MORROW Great story.

You're an avid sailor and golfer. How do those relate to
your success in business?

PLATTNER When we started the company, Dietmar Hopp
told everybody, "We don't go skiing anymore. That's
too risky. We could break our legs, and that could kill
the company." So I stopped skiing. And I went back
to sailing.

The active life

Whenever pressure was high in the company or it was
difficult, I went sailing. I went to regattas. I think during
the years I worked the most hours, I sailed the most
regattas as well.

When you are really active—perhaps it is only true for
me—I cannot stop. I have to do something else. I cannot sit there. I always wished to sit at a lake, with rain
drizzling down, and to fish. A wonderful picture of
patience and tranquility. But I can't do it.

All my life, I've had to do physical exercise with some
technical flavor. I did windsurfing for many years, and I
still do. I windsurfed with the big guys from Hawaii and
in various places in the world. It was a great day for me
in the late 1980s when I sailed with one of the World
Cup surfers in Barbados. We surfed with a windsurfer in
synch, three waves, and did many turns together—perhaps five. I dropped my board at the beach and said,
"That was my best day in windsurfing. I will never be
able to repeat it." Unfortunately, I was right!

I went back to sailing after that. I still do windsurfing
for some physical exercise. But I started big-boat
sailing again.

Hasso Plattner surfing at the end of the 70s.

MORROW Big-boat sailing is certainly real-time information flow and constant activity.

Surfing and snowboarding

PLATTNER Yes, it's a lot of information. It's a technical sport, a concentration sport, and a team sport. And after many, many years, I am now back to winter sports. I do snowboarding. You would never believe it, but just recently I was snowboarding in Aspen, and somebody of my age asked me, "How do you do this?" And I said, "I just started three years ago." And he was shocked. I said, "Yes, but I was a good windsurfer." Because it's very similar to windsurfing. I read in a magazine that Robby Nash from Hawaii, the famous windsurfer, picked up snowboarding within two hours. And within two days, he was ready for competition.

So it took me two days to snowboard, but I'm still not ready for competition. (Laughter.)

Perhaps a metaphor: the Sydney-Hobart race

MORROW Well, I was told that it would be criminal of me to do this interview and not ask you about the Sydney-Hobart record. Will you tell me about that race? It was a nice way to begin the 25th anniversary year; it was December 30.

PLATTNER We were lucky in sailing that day. The Sydney-Hobart race is the biggest sports event in Australia. And there is a record to break—or there was a record to break. And that was the highest prize money in sailing—about 300,000 Australian dollars. And we had two major races last year—Hawaii and San Francisco. And in both races, we broke a mast. So we went to Sydney.

I arrived at 6:00 in the morning. I drove to the hotel, changed, and went to the boat. We went out. We sailed. At 10:30, we broke the mast. The third mast broken within four months.

I reacted in a funny way. I got used to it. We just looked at the mast and sailed the boat home safely. And we were all on the cellular phone talking through the various options of how to get our spare mast, which was still in Auckland, New Zealand. And then the story started. It was on television every day. I could sit there in my hotel room, watch the television, and see what was going on and who was saying where the mast was. Qantas finally flew in the mast. The two pilots had to divert a flight from Hawaii.

A logistical tour de force

It started in Los Angeles, went to Hawaii, had to go to Fiji—but skipped Fiji, went to Auckland, skipped Melbourne, and went directly to Sydney. There was a curfew in Sydney. They landed five minutes before the curfew. There was a big thunderstorm, and they wanted to divert the flight. The pilot said, "We're going to make it. We're going to make it with the mast. We have the mast. We have the mast." They landed at 9:50 P.M.

They took out the mast. It was pouring. Police were ready to help get the mast through the city, and it was on television every minute. They stepped the mast

The *Morning Glory* puts to sea

overnight. The next day, at 10 A.M., we went out sailing to practice again. Helicopters were everywhere, monitoring the *Morning Glory* with a new mast. "Qantas did it. Qantas did it." Great advertising for Qantas.

MORROW Qantas.

PLATTNER I just had to pay for the fuel. Just the kerosene. And the pilots were absolutely fabulous. It was a different experience. We could not get the prime minister to postpone the curfew. But they made it.

Stormy night and a happy voyage

We were experienced racers. I had the best crew ever, perhaps. Two Olympic champions, many world champions, and a lot of miles. And we had an early start on a long-distance race. We had gone back for this repaired mast that had broken three times. Four hours out of Sydney, we hit a big storm. We saw it coming. We didn't believe it because calm weather had been predicted. There was a storm with winds of 40 or 45 knots.

We took the mainsail down to protect our mast. We didn't trust our mast. The boat next to us, the other favorite—actually the race favorite from Australia—boom, they lost their mast. There they went.

We got through the night. The next day, we had fantastic weather, and we went really fast. Nobody really had known how fast we could go. Now they knew. For four hours, we went an average of 22 knots.

MORROW Wow!

PLATTNER With a peak speed of 25 knots. That's fun sailing!

We had the guy from Brazil who had just won the gold medal in Savannah in a Star boat. He was enjoying his life. He said, "That's my best sailing day ever." And we were five hours ahead of schedule.

Becalmed

Then, there was no wind. The last 60 miles are very tricky—up a river, the Derwent, to Hobart.

It was terrible. We were sitting there. And everybody knew we wouldn't make the record. We wouldn't make the record. And I had promised the crew that we would split the money among us if we won. I had made this promise before the mast broke. Some had said, "Don't you want to take the money for the mast?" I said, "No. I'll keep my promise. Come on, guys."

MORROW Oh, fabulous!

PLATTNER So everybody was anxious to win this prestigious award.

MORROW So the wind dies, and you have the hardest three tacks of the race left still to do?

And then we did it

PLATTNER Yes, but with 30 minutes to go, we knew we would make it. And we started very, very calmly to celebrate. But nobody spoke a word. The last two hours, no words were spoken except the commander's commands. There was dead silence on board. And then we made it.

MORROW Wow! Fabulous!

PLATTNER The 21-year-old record. An hour later, I got the fax from Jim Kilroy on *Kialoa III*, cruising in the Caribbean. He was on the telephone all the time, asking, "Did they make it?" He held the record. And then I got the fax, "Congratulations for breaking my record. Kilroy onboard *Kialoa III*." The second to congratulate us was in two hours, Ed Heath, the former prime minister from the UK who won the race in 1977.

MORROW Well, that's a fabulous story.

The happy winners and new record holders of the Sydney-Hobart Regatta (1996).

PLATTNER Before that, nobody in Europe had ever recognized me on an airplane. But when I flew from Hobart back to Sydney, the stewardess said, "Oh, are you Mr. Plattner, who won the Sydney-Hobart race?" Because we had been on television for four days, basically on every newscast.

MORROW What about the America's Cup?

PLATTNER No.

MORROW No?

The America's Cup—I would rather go play golf

PLATTNER No. That type of race is not interesting enough for me. To sail around these buoys. I fell asleep in the finals, when New Zealand won. And actually I missed the most exciting parts, when the girls were leading by four-and-a-half minutes, in front of Paul Cayard. I switched off the television and went golfing. And I said, "The girls made it! The girls made it!" Somebody came up and said, "What are you talking about? The girls didn't make it. Cayard made it." I said, "That's not possible. I saw them leading by miles." "Yes, but he won." The same thing happened to me in 1989 in the world championship in Naples. I was leading or about to lead, at least, the world championship. And then Paul Cayard passed us in a calm. He lured us in. We all stopped. Two boats passed. Then he made it to the finish line. So we finished fourth, instead of first. Paul Cayard did this before. And the girls are still in shock.

I love sailing. I love competing. But it has to be more interesting than just "up and down and up and down and up and down" for a year. I have all the respect for Mr. Koch, who did it in *America3*.

MORROW Well, I have one last question. What would you say to a young person just coming out of the university now and interested in a future in information technology? What would you say about preparation and what

Advice to the next generation

the future would be like? And what do you say to new, young talent when you're trying to convince them that this is the place to be?

PLATTNER There are a lot of reasons to join SAP. But somehow, the flair of the young start-up is gone, and we have difficulties getting the new young renegades off the street and incorporating them.

There is another revolution about to come, and it's an exciting time. It's good to start with a large company. I learned a lot from IBM. And I would not be here without IBM—no question about it. You need more than just talent and spirit. You need some formal education. You have to travel as much as possible, even in your business. All the things we mentioned in this interview are true. And all this contributed to what we are today and how we shaped the company.

The world of tomorrow: open and democratic

It is a global market. This is exciting. But the young kids are global already. They are on the Internet. They all speak English now. They learn. They have figured out, "The only way to communicate with somebody in Hong Kong or in Korea is in English. So we'd better learn English. Otherwise, we cannot read our letters." For them, it is so normal to check out something on the Internet and find something interesting somewhere else in the world.

I think this global world will be our future world. It is very difficult to keep your nationalistic attitude in this global world. I am in favor of an absolutely open Internet. People will take on the responsibility themselves, because of the feedback—the impressive reaction in a democratic society. Democracy means you can express what you want to, you can exchange what you think, and you can find the reaction. There will be a mass reaction, killing the virus of evilness. This is what I believe is exciting. This is different from the time I was born into, starting with Berlin and the Berlin airlift.

All the pressure of our ex-enemies, the Russians, put on us. And, then, all of a sudden, it was gone. It's a different world.

An experience I had recently that really impressed me a lot was at our user conference in South Africa. We had the conference in Lost City, this huge entertainment park close to Johannesburg. There is an artificial beach, and we had a beach party there. Five or six people were standing around. Most of them were Africans, and one was a 6-foot-2-inch or 6-foot-3-inch guy. I asked him, "What are you doing?" He said, "I am a consultant in R/3." I said, "Oh, great. You do R/3 consulting?" "Yes. And I just installed an R/3 system in Pakistan." I said, "You did what?" "I installed an R/3 system in Pakistan." I said, "Wait a minute. You were born in South Africa?" "Yes, in Soweto." "You work for—?" "Siemens." "You do R/3?" "Yes." "You do consulting for R/3 in Pakistan?" "Yes."

Hasso Plattner in conversation with participants at the conference.

Another guy from Kenya started laughing. He said, "Yes, I am from Kenya. I found you on the Internet. I have a little consulting company in Kenya, in Nairobi, and we do R/3. We are practicing. We're trying to get customers in Africa. And then I will expand. I will do consulting in the UK. I will do consulting everywhere. We might not be able to build cars anymore, and perhaps telephone systems are gone, and microchips went to Asia, but we can do consulting. I have an MBA. I started in London. I know the guys. I'm as good as they are."

That guy so impressed me. He said, "I found you on the Internet." And I told him, "You will get a PC system for $8,000 in a few months' time, where everything we have is on the computer and you get everything else on the Internet. So either you have SAP on the Internet, or you have it on this little laptop." And we are shipping this laptop now. That was such a great experience for me. We had never had a business relationship with a 50-person consulting company in Nairobi. They found us on the Internet. He worked out by himself that SAP is the market leader, obviously, and he wanted to do business consulting, so he went for the market leader. And this, I think, is a new kind of opportunity.

For young people in their early 20s, I think there is a great opportunity. Whatever happens 10 years from now, start with a global mind and a global world.

MORROW It's a great time to be alive. And it's a great pleasure to have interviewed someone who not only has made such a great contribution, but who so obviously still enjoys and thrills at the potential of his business. Thank you very much, on behalf of all of us.

Chapter 2

The Beginnings and Turning Points

But to have the sensation itself, the R/3 applications system, in the UNIX world, you concealed that?

We hid it because no one would have understood it.

Walldorf, January 23, 1998

WENDT Let's talk here about visions. Visions are extrapola-
tions from experience and everyone has his own background of experiences. I think it would be interesting
for us to start off by exchanging our backgrounds.
What were the key events in your past and how have
they left their mark? After all, we all played around with
the computer shortly after Zuse had invented it, and
today computing has become a wild area of activity. So
it is interesting what events left their burning marks on
our minds.

Basic technical
experience

Mr. Plattner, the founder of SAP, did his graduate work
with Prof. Steinbuch in Karlsruhe in 1968. He had a lot
to do with software even during his course of studies.

PLATTNER Yes, for my degree work, I had to program and
develop a minimizing-optimizing process for passive
switching circuits. The program that existed at the
Institute ran terribly slowly and there was the hope that
someone could improve on it. What impressed me was
the fact that through one basic change in procedure,
you would effect not just a 10 percent or 20 percent
improvement. There was an order-of-magnitude factor
of 100 between the changed versions, perhaps even
more.

Prof. Dr. August Wilhelm Scheer—Director of the Institute for Wendt.

Director of the Institute for Business Information Science of the University of Saarland and founder and Chairman of the Supervisory Board of the IDS Scheer AG.

WENDT May I bring my memory into play here? Mr. Plattner mentioned that at the time before he did his degree work, the program ran very slowly. I was the author of the program. I had written it for my student assistants, who really needed such a program. So without a great deal of consideration, I wrote a program in Algol with the 08/15 algorithm, which was well known at the time, mentioned in every lecture. I only wanted the experience, and it did not bother me at all that it took the whole night for the thing to run. I would start the program at 7:00 in the evening, and on the next morning at 8:00, I would have the results. When Mr. Plattner was finished with his doctoral work, his advisor, Mr. Beisdorf, came and said to me, "Don't you still have your old jobs that took you an entire night to run? Now let's run the same jobs with Mr. Plattner's program." It took 52 seconds.

Prof. Dr.-Ing. Siegfried Wendt— Managing Director of the Hasso Plattner Institute for Software Systems Technology in Potsdam.

Prof. Hasso Plattner—Speaker for the board of SAP AG.

PLATTNER Yes, referring to Andy Grove's inflection point theory in his book, *Only the Paranoid Survive*, that was just such an inflection point. Through thinking things over and changing procedures, you can achieve more than one factor-10 effect.

SCHEER In what language was the program in Karlsruhe written at that time?

PLATTNER The framework of the program in Karlsruhe was written in Fortran and the core in Assembler and CDC Assembler on a CDC installation. They were logical operations and they were done with the Assembler. It was a 36-bit machine, and because the logical operations should be longer, the first task was to make a 72-bit machine out of a 36-bit machine and to double everything and emulate a 72-bit machine with software by using small macros.

SCHEER Today everyone would laugh at the computers we had available then. I don't know whether it is the same with you, but it seems to me that the basic experiences that we had then, for example, mounting a tape yourself or programming in Assembler, really could not be replaced by anything else.

As if the
machine spoke

PLATTNER Yes, if we stick with the CDC installation at the University of Karlsruhe, for example, I had exactly such basic experiences there. It was really a matter of achieving speed with my program and observing exactly how the program behaved. At that time, there weren't any debuggers, but you could watch the machine. The main memory lay quasi-optically visible before you. You could turn down the speed control, which could be freely regulated, and let the machine work very slowly step-by-step and then again faster and then again slower and then again faster. Because I had the machine freely available, I could really play around with it. That was enormously interesting, and it was almost as if the machine spoke to me. It really showed me where the program was running slowly, just what it was doing, and how the loops functioned. I had a physical impression about how loop programming worked on the computer and how the computer suffered when you write a loop badly.

SCHEER Or the exciting and aesthetic experience of a sort run with six tape machines. Each tape machine was as big as a clothes closet. You noticed that they were all rewinding and then you saw how they were sorting into each other. You really experienced the computer and understood whether everything was running properly.

At IBM at
that time

PLATTNER After my studies, I went to IBM and it was exactly the opposite there. The first practical job on an IBM computer was a contrast program. This super-fast new IBM computer had, by the way, the dimensions of a MIPS. The machine came new to IBM, and then I went with one of the chief system engineers to the Bundesanstalt der Länder, BLA, in Karlsruhe. We had to convert some output formats and I thought, "Well, we'll do that now." Then the system engineer said, "No, no, we will prepare it. We need 10 of them; we will prepare all of them first, we will check again to see whether everything is properly defined, we will put it into the machine, and then we will go get something to eat." And I said, "What will we do?" "Then we will get something to eat." So we got something to eat and then some more to eat and we had a beer, and then we returned and looked at what had become of our conversion. It was not a program, but just a definition that you could use later somewhere in a program. This experience gave me quite a shock and almost prompted me to leave IBM after six weeks. It was all very mechanical, what they were doing. This led to the starting point of SAP.

I took over the administration of the IBM library from Dietmar Hopp, and when I was not fully occupied, I worked on putting the library in order, so I was always reading. I read about the machines in America, the largest existing computers of IBM or the famous computers that never made it. For example, the system 67 was the first multiprocessor machine with virtual memory and parallel processing. Then, there was also the Model 91; it was supposed to put CDC out of the running in large scientific applications. These computers were depicted with overall good documentation, and I absorbed all of it. I learned what the inside of a typical IBM computer looks like, and then the first terminals and screens already began to appear. With these, we also started to program a little and then came—also through the literature—the 3270 terminal.

That was the decision point, and I believe that the entire DP industry started anew on that day. The 3270 had a screen 80 lines horizontal and 24 rows vertical. The 80 lines come from the punched-card technology, 24 punched cards one above the other. In any case, the so-called tabulator control let you control the individual

The decision point—the 3270 terminal

field points on the screen. You could also assign for-mats. It was thus a format-controlled screen. That was the breakthrough because you could figure on a certain local intelligence or readiness. You could navigate over this screen rapidly and enter data, revolutionizing the entire I/O process—the flow of the data from the busi-ness administration departments into the computer and then back.

The old classical method was to write it down, translate it into the punched-card formulas, punch the cards, check them out, run them in the computer, and print out the famous white-and-green striped endless lists, which were distributed at headquarters at an end. That was substantially my experience with IBM, and it was also the starting point for SAP. The entire technology invented there greatly improved for quite a while as performance increased and main memory grew larger and larger, but everything relied on the basic principle that all the memory, drives, and processes for multiple users would be developed on one computer, in one entity, and in one operating system. It was a design in which the users were brought to the computer, and the logical processing was done there.

This principle held out for a long time. We basically dropped it only in 1990 when central computers could no longer keep up with the growth rate of our applica-tions. You have to imagine that by the end of the 1980s, the largest systems were running with thou-sands, even tens of thousands, of users on a single physical installation. At this time, it would have four to six processors, but no more than that. You were very limited with this computer architecture, and we broke through in almost a single act of doubt and said, "Now we have to try what SUN has already begun in the sci-entific field, computing on a large number of comput-ers, that is, distributing the applications over a large number of computers."

WENDT Well, the first machine that I programmed was the Z22 from Zuse. The first computer language that I learned—and that first language leaves a lasting impression—was Algol. Later, in my practicum at IBM, I got acquainted with the Assembler 1620 from IBM. I was given to the Porsche company by IBM as an advertising gift, that is, I was paid by IBM. I was supposed to program in the engineering office at Porsche, and there I implemented the entire floating-decimal arithmetic on the IBM 1620 with software because it wasn't there on the hardware. This also made a big impression.

Programming as an occult science

In fact, I thought of myself as a guru at that time, whereas today I give such gurus a hard time. The programming was tricky and we had little working memory; I didn't care anything at all about documentation and had everything in my head. I was quite proud of the fact that after I left Porsche, I got a call from there saying, "Mr. Wendt, in your programs—not that there are any mistakes in them—but we would like to add a supplemental function and so on and so on and we don't understand this or that. . . ." I was quite proud that I could tell these people over the phone just how to do it.

SCHEER That was the ambition at that time, to write every program in three lines. The programmer as alchemist whom no one understands—nor should they understand him because that would mean that he would lose his aura. This was completely opposed to today's principles of software technology.

WENDT Yes, completely nuts. I naturally learned Fortran at IBM as well and returned to the university, which had the ER-56 from SEL. That is a fully transistorized computer, with germanium transistors in part, but very sensitive to temperature. In the entire university, only 10 people could program at the Assembler level. When you got the computer . . . that is, I got it, no one else could have it, and I operated it the same way you

An operating system—how stupid!

would a rental car and said, "Either you have it or I do, but we can't both have it." That is how you worked with that computer.

And then I experienced—this was interesting—how Steinbuch's assistants wired in the interruption capability in this computer after the fact. It had not been there before. One assistant, Wettstein by name, went to IBM in America for half a year, came back, and said that they were making operating systems there. Just think, we had loaded our programs in the naked, empty working memory. Other than our program, there was nothing in there, nothing at all!

He came back and said that they have operating systems. Then he, too, wrote an operating system and named it Betsy (for BETriebsSYstem [operating system]); this made all of us furious because he had taken away our right to be the only ones giving commands to this computer. Suddenly someone with his own program prevented us from being able to do all the great things that we had been doing. How we cursed that Wettstein with his stupid operating system that no one needed at all. I still remember just exactly how things were.

In contrast, you can see today that without the basic idea of a change of context in the computer, you could not produce essential things. Just today in my lecture, I presented the grandiose idea of a change in context. When I am sitting down and working on something and the telephone rings—Pow!—there is a change of context and I ask, "Who is on the phone and what do I have to do?" Or there is a knock at the door. Or I am writing a letter and my pencil breaks.

PLATTNER It became a great problem again 15 years later with the PCs. Not such a long time ago, you could either type or print on Windows-based PCs, but you could not continue to type while it was printing. The operating system could not make the change in context and do two things in parallel.

SCHEER Yes, clearly. It was practically the same principle. In my recollections, it is clear that a computer must have a teak cabinet because the first computer on which I worked, the TR-4—the TR stood for Telefunken Computer (Rechner, in German)—was covered in teak wood and stuck in my mind. There were no programming instructions; instead, we had just five pages about Algol that had been copied under the table and were handled as something precious. But the computers were good for some things, even then. I still remember one Univac computer that was water-cooled, and you could put your beer bottles in there to keep them cold.

From the early years of data processing

Then as an assistant, I learned for the first time just what data processing is. I had already learned programming as a student around 1963. Actually, I hardly studied at all and did not earn a single grade honestly because I was always programming for some other department; back then, that was worth something. They would give me the grades for that, and all I had to take was my final exams. I made out real well in that.

Then I was an assistant at the Institute for Operations Research and got the job of developing a system for the distribution of medical students among the universities, the forerunner to the present day ZVS. At that time, the Numerus Clausus was organized by each individual university, and there were duplicate applications because the same students were accepted at several universities. We had to develop a system to sort this out. For the first time I saw, after only programming algorithms, that you can have more than 20 data sets. Suddenly, I had to handle thousands of data sets. We worked with magnetic tape then, and the quality of the sorting algorithms determined whether a run would take five hours or half an hour. There were efficiency criteria that you did not get to know at all with purely algorithmic programming. For me, that was the entry point into data processing.

There were stories about programming at night in the computer room; I can relate to them quite well. I remember well how I was stuck there from 5 p.m. to 7 a.m. The period ended at 7:00 in the morning for maintenance time, when the computer was shut down. You had to organize your program to finish up in two hours. The guy before me was assigned 3:00. At that time, he stood up with his box of punched cards to enter the computer room to read them in. But he caught the sleeve of his jacket on the door handle and the whole stack of punched cards went flying across the computer room; he finally just went home.

German
computer
technology

These were the kinds of things that made data processing somehow a personal matter. When I think about the TR-4 and the TR-440, also an operating system . . . in my opinion, the TR-440 operating system was world-class for that time. So there remains the question: What has happened with German computers?

WENDT For my doctoral thesis, I did simulations on the TR-4. I had the same experience with the teakwood computer, and I observed that the Algol compiler was excellent. With three runs, I tested and corrected my large-scale program, and then I could run simulations the entire year without encountering any additional problems. I attribute that to the excellent Algol compiler, which would produce a post-mortem dump. When the program crashed while running, it printed out at a symbolic level: The program failed on line X of the procedure, which was called by the following parameters from procedure Y, and so on. That means that you could read the dump and know exactly what had gone wrong. Fantastic! Three runs, three dumps, and all the errors had been found. That was excellent operating-system software.

SCHEER The German computers are extinct, but what has not disappeared is the know-how that was acquired then because a number of the developers who worked in Konstanz at the time went into higher education. I'm thinking of Professors Hotz and Jessen. The know-how went into information technology research in Germany. It is too bad, in my opinion, that not enough came back out. Science was made out of the products, but no new products then came back out of the science. That is a real shame when you take another look at it.

WENDT At the time, there were only two computer companies in Germany. Zuse was one and it was quickly bought up by Siemens, and then Telefunken and Siemens built computers. Siemens stayed in the business—at the time it had the Siemens 2002 series—but very soon Siemens joined forces with RCA. The Siemens 3003 series, when you opened up the cabinet, was really an RCA machine with a Siemens label.

SCHEER What we are discussing are mostly boxes and abstract concepts, but behind these are the people who brought them to life. People who perhaps were not able to make their ideas into reality on the first try and who looked for compromises between a fascination with technology and profitability—but who also fought not to go along with every trend of the technology. It is also crazy that this whole technology has developed so furiously in the past 30 to 40 years, but certain basic matters have remained strangely constant. For example, the Von Neumann principle.

WENDT Yes.

SCHEER When something tips things so much that the foundation stone begins to wobble?

WENDT What changes rapidly over time, what changes very slowly, and what remains the same?

Is there such a thing as ultimate knowledge?

And there are simply basic principles that persist. Nobody has any grounds for thinking about changes or sees a weak point anywhere, so they persist. For example, when we switched over from Roman numerals to the Arabic numbers, the decimal point came with it and so it remains today. The matter was closed. Today no one has an idea that something is wrong and that we still have to change something.

But the binary number system rests upon the same principle! It is just the conversion from base 10 to base 2. The basic idea that each position has its potential value did not change.

It is the same with the Von Neumann principle. At the beginning, it was still being disputed. The first Zuse computer was not developed according to the Von Neumann principle, but rather the program was in a different technology from that of a data storage memory. You could take the film strips, punch holes in them, and then go back and forth. That is, the operand memory was technologically separated from the program memory. And this concept of separation hindered the semantic leap. That is the recognition that someone had and that then persisted, namely that information is neither eternally program or operand but is sometimes program and sometimes operand. What the compiler produces is not program, but operand. Suddenly, however, someone says that it should be program—that is, it should control the machine, and we don't want for it to be changed technologically and transported somewhere else.

This simply means that we take off the glasses through which we were viewing it as operand, put on other glasses, and say, "Now it is program!" This assumes that we do not have any technological separation between the operand memory and the program memory. This recognition will persist and in a thousand years will be the same. After all, the technology of our brain is the same. Noting lexical knowledge—for example, how many inhabitants Moscow has—is the same as noting how to ski. But skiing is a program; it is controlling.

I do not expect that the Von Neumann principle will ever disappear, even in a thousand years. Just as our way of thinking about numbers will never disappear. So for me some things are final knowledge, ultimate knowledge.

PLATTNER Hm, hm.

SCHEER Mr. Wendt, how did you first come into contact with SAP?

First encounter with SAP

WENDT I made contact with SAP truly by coincidence. I don't know whether you still remember, Mr. Plattner, how that contact came about.

In April 1990, I got a message from my secretary, "A Mr. Plattner from SAP called and wanted something from you, but he didn't want to tell me what. He wants to talk with you. He left a number for you to call him back." At that time, I had already been on the Computer Commission of the DFG for nine years and therefore already knew that SAP was a software company. But I did not know where it was located, how big it was, and what kind of software it produced. No idea. I had no idea that this Mr. Plattner had anything to do with it.

The last time that I had seen Mr. Plattner was in spring of 1969 when we were working at the same institute in Karlsruhe. I had graduated and left the institute. Mr. Plattner had done his graduate work there and had also left. Since that time, we had not seen each other again. And that was a good 21 years before. It therefore had not rung any bell when the secretary said Mr. Plattner.

I called back, everything came back to me, and I remembered. And what did he want? He only wanted the curriculum for our department because he was a member of the board of trustees for establishing an information technology department at Mannheim. As thorough as he is, he had collected the relevant curricula from all over Germany. This is how he came to me. Just before we ended our conversation, he asked me, "So what else are you doing? Are you still working on your control loops from back then?" I replied, "I do something with them in my teaching, but for 15 years now I have been modeling complex software." Then he said, "Oh, I am interested in that! I'll stop by sometime."

The interpreter concept

Three days later, he appeared with Mr. Rodé and we talked. Then we did a small project together, and from that an intensive collaboration came about. He recognized that the R/3 needed someone, a modeler and abstracter, to produce ongoing documentation so that the technical structure would be more evident. The R/3 largely developed from a technological standpoint, and you can very easily get lost. What he did not want was only 10 gurus, and no one else, knowing what the system looks like. That meant that I looked into the heart of the R/3—into the dispatcher, the task handler, and the interpreter—very intensively. I read the sources and I was very impressed by certain decisions about the architecture. What I learned at the time, for example, and where I previously had had my doubts, was that an interpretation—every ABAP processor is after all an interpreter—can be performed at all! I then executed the interpreter loops in code myself and recognized that the interpreter is not a bottleneck.

PLATTNER Today everyone talks about a "virtual machine."

WENDT It took me a long time to learn what advantages the interpreter concept has.

SCHEER I remember very well when I first heard the name SAP. It was in 1980 on a consulting project at the company Villeroy & Boch, which was considering using standard software. The discussion was still going on over standard software and specialized development. Then someone from SAP came to Saarbrücken to see me at the institute, but he was not especially eager to come; I had to call three times before he agreed that he should be involved in such a selection process, no matter how interesting it was.

I recall like it was today that he had a schematic of a kind of data model with him. What really impressed me was that this data model clearly showed the parallel nature of the procurement field and the sales field because approximately the same concepts show up in both areas. With sales, it is called "customers" and with procurement, it is "suppliers," but in both areas there are accounts, reminders, stipulations, and so on. The similarity of structure was clear.

The integration design

I suddenly saw: This is a new approach to thinking about business administration! Apply the integration concept to operational processes that belong both to sales in value-derived information like debit accounting and to procurement in credit accounting. I also thought about our business administration; in the basic studies, I had advocated some discussion of finance accounting, but afterwards in the treatment of operational things like logistics, we did not further discuss the value level. These two things, the integration and also the formal presentation, that is, the use of models, made me interested in SAP.

In 1975, when I came to Saarbrücken and took over the chair for economic information science, I read the book by Wedekind on data bank systems, which covered the first usage of relational data models, and I read Peter Chen's 1975 essay "Towards a Unified View on Data," which presented the entity relationship model. These new views of business administration attracted me to SAP.

The use of dialogue in accounting

A second occasion that I remember well was when Mr. Plattner appeared at the Saarbrücken Working Conference, around the beginning of the 1980s. He gave a paper on the subject "The Use of Dialogue in Accounting." About 400 experts from industry and science took part in the conference, which was quite a few for that time. Mr. Plattner presented the first concepts for cost accounting in dialogue. Mr. Plaut was also present and he spoke out vehemently against such concepts. In the discussions, he argued that accounting is tied to periods of time and you close the accounts once a month or once a year. Why would you then need an ongoing processing dialogue? At the most, you could use it for core data maintenance, but otherwise, the procedures are based on periods and thus predestined for batch processing.

Tools and methods

What came through in these arguments was how easy it is to forget about the dependency between tools and methods. That is, traditional accounting was oriented toward its tools, namely pencil and paper. With these tools, it took a terribly long time to complete a calculation, so you did it only once a year. It was not that you did not otherwise have an interest in the information, such as how much a product cost! That means that when the tools suddenly change, the business administration methods also change, and you no longer do things only once a year or once a month, but you do them when someone has an interest in them! And this can mean that in a bank, you might want to see a balance every second and not only once a year. This interaction between tools and business administration procedures was apparent.

I still exactly recall the answer to Mr. Plaut's question, "Mr. Plattner, why are you doing dialogue processing?" After perhaps one second's hesitation, he said,

Institute for Business Information Science in Saarbrücken.

"Because we can do it!" That is, the technology is now here and we have to rethink how we will set up the procedures to make effective use of this technology.

From these first contacts, we developed a collaboration of many years in areas such as modeling the business administration content of the R/3 system or new logistics concepts. The lectures by Mr. Plattner at the University of Saarbrücken were also a result of this. They satisfied Mr. Plattner's interest in university research and teaching, but I saw them above all as a chance to present the students with a personality from the new high-tech founders scene, in addition to the technical content of the lectures. They should be guided by the fascination with and commitment to new ideas and introduce these experiences into their own attitudes toward life.

Now that we have taken a look at the early days of data processing, let's return to the development from central computers to the computer networks about

Centralization and decentralization

which Mr. Plattner was just speaking. From an organizational theory standpoint, this is a change from the centralized form of organization to the decentralized form of organization. In organizational theory, centralization and decentralization are well-known phenomena with certain characteristics.

With centralization, for example, coordination is simple, and you know exactly where the data and programs are located; everything is simply in one box. Decentralization, by contrast, requires considerable coordination, because otherwise you cannot direct the individual units towards a common goal, towards common task implementation. In certain situations, organizational centralization is good, and in certain situations, decentralization is preferable. You can play around with these concepts, depending on what you are trying to do.

What was the decisive point in the changeover from the central R/2 system to the decentralized R/3 system? Was it only performance considerations that forced a move from centralization to decentralization, or was it the user businesses who wanted to decentralize themselves organizationally and therefore needed information systems that could be deployed in a decentralized manner—or was it both?

The basic decision on the R/3: IMS and the principle of parallelism

PLATTNER I think that these two things are always mixed up with each other or brought into a false relationship with each other—the decentralized principle of organization in the business and the centralized or decentralized processing in a system. Let's go back a step. In the 80s, we started to build IMS-based systems for our larger customers. IMS was a data and transaction processing system under which our applications programs ran.

IMS was the IBM software system that had been thought through the most thoroughly, by a long shot. Because it had been designed so well, it was also relatively powerful and had always been received with hostility by the other developments that then needed narrower solutions, such as the English CICS. What was the essence of this IMS system? It was based on a data bank, and the data bank ran in one logical section, called a partition. Independently, there was a transaction control mechanism and the applications ran in yet another partition of their own. By the way, today you would probably say this was a process, rather than a partition, even though they are not quite the same.

In any case, the inventors of IMS had foreseen that multiple users would want to use a certain application, and therefore an application must be running on a computer multiple times simultaneously. You had to be able to let multiple users work in parallel in a single application. This parallel working brings some complexities with it, however, such as the synchronization between the applications partitions. They cannot access the same data set for data entry at the same time.

All these things that are self-evident for us today were considered by IBM as far back as the early 70s, and when we were building the R/3, we reached back for this experience. At the time, I put out the word that our target system is not CICS, but rather nothing other than IMS. IMS is our target system and if we are diverted from IMS to other systems, then IBM should set things up with their project at that time, the SAA project. In this integration project, IMS was involved early and CICS was not included. This was a broad hint from IBM that I gratefully picked up. What did that mean for our development? With the intellectual IMS concept, we could work in a strong parallel manner because we needed multiuser systems for a large number of users.

We needed a designation to help us imagine the architecture: to have an application on the computer multiple times that can work on the same data bank. With this architecture, you can serve a very large number of users if the computer is big enough, because the operating system of these parallel working partitions in the

Scalability

IMS system is reflected in the physical computer. A computer has, let us say, 8 registers with 16 such partitions. With an increase in the size of the computer, this principle can grow further and the number of partitions can be increased. This logical concept was a rethinking of the CICS concept where all the users are brought to a program and a queue builds up waiting for it. Only late in the 1980s did CICS get to the point where they could put two CICSs alongside each other so that they could communicate. But previously, CICS did not foresee parallel working.

SCHEER What comes through very clearly here is that with the SAP applications system, you were deeply bound into the system architecture so that the operating system, data bank system, and transaction monitor, even, practically lived with the hardware and system software.

PLATTNER . . . always lived with it, but not for the reasons of the early years of data processing, because it was so much fun to work that way, but rather because the roots of the system design were found there. The parallel nature was obviously the key to how you could build any large or super-large computers at all. To understand the meaning of this, let's jump back to the early years again.

A CICS experience

In the 1980s, we already had experience with large systems; here is a CICS experience on the subject. It was around the end of the time when Dietmar Hopp and I were programming. We got called to the Philips company in Hamburg. A SAP system installed there was getting more unstable every day, and the dumps—the printed memory extracts after the system had crashed—filled an entire conference room. While we were there, new ones were printing all the time. It was an absolute crisis. What had happened? At the time, all our applications and all our users simultaneously occupied a large address room in the system, and if anything went wrong, they could affect one another.

We had developed a small routine for some kind of data transfer for Philips. This routine had an error and, practically through an accidental algorithm, changed one byte, 8 bits, in the main memory. When it did this the first time, it did not cause much trouble; the second time, still maybe not; but subsequently, the change did cause trouble because the system crashed. They were able to restart the system and keep it running. However, the routine caused changes in data that was later written back to the external disks, and that meant that the error became permanent. Finally over 14 days, the system made itself sick; it contracted a virus. There were computer viruses even back then. Viruses destroy not only the temporary data in the main memory, but also the persistent data. The error was catastrophic.

Thank God that we knew the system so well back then that after about two or three hours, we identified approximately where the error was coming from. After a day, we found the error and immediately corrected the program, and there were no more new crashes. However, a lot of data had been infected somehow, where a string of 8 bits had been changed, and it took weeks to find all the erroneous data.

Separation of
the applications

This interdependence within the R/2 system was a great weakness. One bad part could affect all the users, because we operated with more and more integration and brought more and more applications together. The R/2 system was already quite large from the standpoint of the applications inventory and was constantly getting bigger, so an error function in any application could eventually threaten all other applications. We did not have any separation of the applications from each other and particularly no separation of potential errors.

In contrast, the parallel operating model of the IMS not only let you include different users on the same data bank, but it also screened off the individual user groups from each other. The operating system made sure that none of these message-processing regions could impact each other; they could only communicate with the other regions through regulated communications, through a so-called message. You thus could not directly get into the main memory of the other regions.

SCHEER But that actually means that the architecture of SAP was created through this coincidence, that you settled on IMS and not on the smaller IBM computers that ran CICS and DL 1. This was practically the parallel to IMS for the smaller IBM operating system DOS.

PLATTNER We did both for the R/2, but as far as the R/3 architecture was concerned, I settled on IMS; otherwise, the R/3 architecture would not have turned out the way it did. When we began to design the R/3 on the blackboard in 1987, I was quite clearly a fan of IMS and was able to convince all the UNIX people who collected around me that IMS is a clear concept, that you can fill in afterwards, and that it has a certain aesthetic: the separation of the purely terminal dialogue traffic from the rest, the separation of the data bank, and the creation of separate units in which the applications run. You can freely choose the organization of the units; that is, each of these units can either do a specific type of application or a type of application can be running in parallel multiple times. Thus we had a construction model. When you now consider that you can run not just 16 in parallel, but 200 or more at a time, this makes quite an impression.

The beginning and the end of the R/3 on the mainframe

This is how we built the system. We also tackled the first unification of applications and base code on an IBM mainframe under MVS/IMS (MVS was the operating system and IMS the applications management system) and then came the shock: It did not work.

Why didn't it work? At the time, we had 80 developers who wanted to do tests; our largest computer had four powerful IBM 3090 processors, and it was the highest performance computer in the north Baden area. Now there can be a lot of errors, and to find an error in the programming language C—we wrote all our technology software in C—there were procedures in IMS. Namely, one CPU could not work for multiple users or for multiple programs simultaneously, but rather briefly one after the other through a change in context. When a C programmer wanted to search for an error, the operating system or IMS automatically set aside a physical processor in the hardware and said, "This belongs to me now and now you can debug."

You can imagine what happened. The first UNIX programmer got an error and called up the debugger, the processor stopped, and Mr. Mattheis, chief of accounting, said, "Today the computer is slow again." Then a second programmer found an error, turned on the debugger and looked at his program, and moved back and forth in steps; in Mr. Mattheis's department, people looked at each other again and said, "Let's go to lunch because things won't get any better today." But two of the processors were still running, so the other developers could always test something that was not as dependent on the response time. But in the professional applications, you noticed the response times.

One-third of the 80 developers also searched for an error, and then the other developers started grumbling that nothing was working. The result was that the entire administration of SAP stopped and the R/2 developers, about 200 people more, threw in the towel. A crisis situation, an absolute catastrophe.

It took a while before we found out what was happening. Every time one of our new UNIX lads searched for an error in a C program and the so-called C debugger switched on, one of our processors stopped. So we recognized the problem; we needed parallel working. We had a requirement that multiple developers wanted to debug their programs, but the operating system and IMS were not capable of it. That was the end of R/3 on the mainframe. We could have waited two years for IBM to fix the debugger, but that is not a simple matter.

WENDT Oh, yes, debugging in a multiplex environment; that takes a long time and it is crazy.

The other approach: SUN

PLATTNER Now comes the decisive question: Just what makes it easier to work in parallel? I believe that this was when we recognized that we had reached the limit in large multiuser operating systems, and we looked for another approach. The other approach was SUN, the Stanford University Network, whose founder was Andy von Bechtholsheim. You had multiple computers, the computers had a much more primitive operating system, and each computer serves only one user or a few users. You therefore do not have a large-scale complicated relationship. This means that the entire system will again be very simple, but the individual computers work in concert and the application must be designed differently to work through a couple of so-called middleware assisting programs. They have to work on a distributed basis.

We were familiar with the concept, and we had also read about it, and several of our newer people had already worked on SUN networks at the university before coming to SAP. A few had worked in the UNIX field at Siemens, so overnight we switched over and said, "It isn't working because this relatively good IMS software concept does not function as a physical implementation on the big computer with the limited hardware." If the 3090 at that time had 32 processors, we would have noticed the problem much later. If the debugger had taken over the computer for only a short time, perhaps two or three seconds, then it would have managed things itself and let others in; the R/3 history would have taken another course. We would have stuck with the mainframe. A totally different R/3 story unfolded instead.

One computer in this network acts as a data bank computer; many other computers play the role of message-processing regions a la IMS, and we call them applications computers; so we need yet another computer type, the communications computer that controls the network and controls the terminals. Instead of terminals, we should use PCs in an active system and no longer work passively, as with the 3270. These terminals did in fact have a small chip inside, but they were not computers in the true sense. On this network, we installed the same logical architecture that we had already used with IMS, which had failed us on the mainframe, and we noted a couple of effects that have persisted until today.

Computer center of SAP after expansion of the buildings on Max Planck Street (1986).

Let's assume that we could have kept this number of applications computers fairly high—for example, 10 applications computers—and we could have served the same number of users as with a typical R/2 system, that is, with a CICS D1-R/2 system. Let's assume that we had 1,000 users. Then we would have had to build an administrative system within the R/2 system to get a thousand users through a bottleneck in the applications. In an R/3 system, we would only have to set up and manage one-tenth as many computers, that is, 10 times 100 users. We learned years ago that a queue grows exponentially with an increase in the number of users. That is, the queuing problem with 3 users is not really a queuing problem, with 30 it becomes somewhat more complicated, and with 3,000 you run into extreme waiting times. This is the main thrust of my applications architecture lectures at the University of Saarland, to demonstrate how this works.

What actually takes place in a computer when too many users come to one physical unit with their applications requirements? We could dramatically simplify the entire management and scheduling. We could assume that we will never have more than 1,000 or 10,000 users, but rather at most 50 to 200 users per applications server. We calculated that when we have 500 users, we need at least two such applications servers, and when we have 1,000 users, then we need perhaps 5 to 10 such applications servers. So we constructed a network: In the center is the data bank system, which continues to be a centralized approach to the data bank, while the applications no longer run on this central computer, but rather all around as applications servers for the data bank computer.

Scheer So you started again with the distribution of functions over various computers—which normally leads to increased complexity because you need a coordination mechanism—but in this case, the individual subsystem could be kept simple?

PLATTNER Yes!

SCHEER We know that we will never get a thousand users on it and we don't need to achieve certain goals, certain performance considerations.

PLATTNER Instead of optimizing the operations system and inventing and optimizing new priority controlling systems, we dramatically reduce the complexity. We use parallel working to do this, something that has long been recognized in production. We did not want to squeeze the last bit out of the production line and pay a high technological price to get 10 percent faster. For years, that was the IBM policy, to make the computer a little faster and a little faster. We wanted parallelism and we put in a second production line alongside. But the way that the users see it, they work in a synchronous manner, and it was always a total system.

So that was the essential change, and it has nothing to do with the decentralized organization of a company. It is still a centralized system, more easily controlled through the overall simplification and the parallel working of the decentralized capacity.

R/3 is a centralized system

SCHEER But this did not fit in exactly with the organizational movements in the businesses that also wanted decentralized systems for organizational reasons. The plants wanted their own systems and did not want to continue to depend on the powerful "DP giants" in the overall business. Can you even say after the technical explanation that the R/3 system was misunderstood to be an organizationally decentralized system?

PLATTNER Yes!

SCHEER Because from a technical viewpoint, it was decentralized, but from the organizational viewpoint, it was still a centralized system—but the user was first of all interested in the organizational decentralization?

PLATTNER Now comes the beauty of the approach. The system can be variably configured, and right from the start, we made it possible to configure the system very small. The minimal configuration was a data bank program, an applications program, and a communications program on a single computer. We can also set it up on a single computer as if we had three computers; that is, the minimal R/3 system was a very small system and today is so small that it will run on a laptop. The entire R/3 system runs on a single laptop, and on the other end of the scale, it goes clearly beyond the maximum expansion range of the R/2 system. In 1993, it was already obvious that the R/3 would be more widely scalable than the R/2, and today we have unbelievably large scaling.

IMS versus
UNIX **SCHEER** The inflection point: The transition from R/2 to R/3 also worked dramatically in the business. Many developers who had previously been assigned to IMS suddenly had to switch over to UNIX. So there was a lot happening in the business.

PLATTNER Yes, the situation was truly dramatic. When we first decided on IMS, the UNIX programmers said, "Well, that's it. I can't work here any more, and I have to look for another job." The R/2 people in SAP said, "So the R/3 won't amount to anything, and we will continue to work on the R/2." At that time, we were putting together the big release 5.0. Its higher functions content had such a strong push back into the R/2 that, except for a small group, everyone lost faith in the R/3.

At a famous crisis meeting, the hard core of the R/3-based development gathered at Daimler Street. I said, "Well, the Hannover Fair can carry us until we can't go any further. There are only six weeks left. We will get the IMS-based R/3 system without any further testing because we can't, after all, cripple the entire SAP. We can't get the system into a presentable state." Everyone also agreed that we would have to give up on the

Dr. Peter Zencke, a member of the board since 1993.

CeBIT. That was the day I stood with my back to the wall and said, "The R/3 project has actually failed."

Then my colleague Peter Zencke—we were at the time, together with Gerd Oswald, the project steering committee for the R/3—said, "Perhaps it has not failed completely. Do we have an alternative?" Let's review things: We got rid of the IBM-SAA and got a C compiler for the basis development, we had the SQL data bank, and we had built a system with a relatively complicated processing technology that was supposed to run under IMS. The applications would be developed on the IMS computer. So we designed the applications in ABAP and the technology in C. We employed a UNIX computer to develop the C routines, but later they were to run under IMS in the production mode.

Necessity is the mother of invention: the R/3 on UNIX

Peter Zencke said, "Instead of putting the basis routines in the mainframe, maybe we could put the applications on the UNIX computer." To which I replied, "Okay, we put the basis routines on one of the largest computers in the world, and now you want to put this huge application on a workstation?" We had DEC 5000 workstations with 25 MIPS. We had just received them a few days before. Still, the workstation is quite a fast computer; it had 25 MIPS and the mainframe had only 20 to 25 MIPS. You can argue about whether mainframe MIPS and RISC MIPS are comparable. But excitement broke out in the room. Perhaps it could work. And then I said, "But Mr. Zencke, we cannot get it done before the Hannover Fair." But then all the employees said, as in a chorus, "Let us try!"

Theoretically, we had the system already appropriately designed. The application does not know the computer; it just works on the ABAP. ABAP is a virtual machine concept; that is, it does not know what the real computer is. We had written the ABAP interpretation in C, and from that we knew that it would run on the DEC workstation. It had been developed on it.

I turned around and said, "Well, good night, gentlemen." It was about 10 p.m. "That's enough for me for today, and I'm going home." I turned back around and saw everyone jump all at once on the DEC workstation;

Gerhard Oswald, member of the board since 1996.

someone grabbed the keyboard and then someone else wanted to get hold of it. They all were shouting, "Come on, let me on, let me on!"

Six weeks later, Gerd Oswald presented the R/3 system at the Hannover Fair. He is a master at showing what is working and avoiding what is not working. He talked and talked and talked, and this DEC workstation was running at the Hannover Fair. The only lie was that it was R/3 running there. We lied when we said that the R/3 is in Walldorf on the mainframe and what we have here is only the terminal, a UNIX terminal. The truth was that the entire R/3 system was running locally in this small machine.

The R/3 at the Hannover Fair

SCHEER But to have the sensation itself, the R/3 applications system, in the UNIX world, you concealed that?

PLATTNER We hid it because no one would have understood it.

The dramatic nature of the leap can only be understood by those who lived in the world of the big mainframe at that time. One day later at the Hannover Fair, I bought 200 HP machines that each had 50 MIPS, twice that of the DEC workstations. We hooked all of them together in Walldorf, and thus in essence each developer got his own workstation. Then we converted the concept from IMS in another six weeks onto this network, and each of these HP workstations was practically an applications server on which one or more developers worked. All of them worked on a single central data bank, our development and test data bank. We built a development system first for 100, then 200, and finally 2,000 developers that had the same architecture as our later production system.

People truly thought things over day and night and also believed that we had to distribute even more, to get away from a mainframe-oriented central repository to a distributed repository. But we did not get to that

The repository: central or distributed

point, certainly not in six weeks. And history has in fact shown that others also did not achieve a distributed repository. We reached a decision pretty soon, in May sometime: "Forget all that with the distribution; along with a central data bank, we will also have a central repository."

This led us to a really great discovery, which for six or seven years was the only one of its kind in the world. It was, "We are writing a system that has a central repository, but we will automatically distribute all the repository elements such as images, programs, and data definitions to all the applications servers. And when there is a change, these changes will automatically be implemented. That is, every developer and every user will know that he is working with the latest version of the repository, and all the synchronization work will automatically be done by the system." This was something that only today—that is, in the last two years—has been achieved by Java.

The master in client/server computing

At that time, we made a technological leap, out of necessity. Perhaps we would not have made it in this way if it had not come out of this necessity. The combination of new technology with a program written in ABAP on the mainframe did not work, but it worked on a logically equivalent system of a workstation network. So if you look at it closely, it is logically a true equivalent to the IMS system. The network is not controlled by an operating system, but rather by our middleware that lies between the operating system and the applications. In 1992 and 1993, our competitors in America, whether it was Oracle or PeopleSoft, who felt that they were already the masters in the client/server environment, laughed at this system because they thought that there were only two possibilities, a fat client or a fat server.

Oracle and PeopleSoft followed the fat client concept. They loaded the applications on the client, and behind this was a thin data bank. This was actually a new concept for PC networks, and when we had our first contact with Bill Gates in 1993, he stated, "Whatever happens in the three-level client/server concept, it must come from the mainframe." The same Bill Gates then three years later in his lectures proclaimed, "Microsoft is building technology software for three-level client/server applications." Larry Ellison of Oracle announced that the new technology from Oracle was a three-level client/server, and Dave Duffield of PeopleSoft said that they were also making a three-level client/server. They had completely redesigned their applications technology. Five years later, our concept had become the standard.

We had worked our way out of this tight situation at the time with all its snags in only 12 weeks. When everyone was talking about client/server, we could join the discussion. At first, everyone thought that client/server was only suitable for smaller companies. Chevron was the first to break through this thinking and understand that client/server was also suitable for larger businesses. Chevron looked at the R/3 system, sized it up, put an incredible amount of business expenditures into it, and finally determined, "The R/3 system has the potential of beating our mainframe."

SCHEER It was always fascinating for me to see how SAP deals with new technologies. Not go along with every fashionable new wave, but stay with stable trends. This has sometimes led to reproaches, but I believe that this art of knowing exactly where I can trust a technology and where I hold off—because I don't want to receive an award for information technology from some people who themselves have never had to invest a single dollar—this art, I believe, is quite visible here. They did not say, "I will build here the first real distributed system in the world," but rather, "I will take the basic idea of a technology and put it into practice."

The right thing at the right time

Bill Gates and Hasso Plattner after signing the contract on collaboration in porting R/3 to Windows NT in April 1993 in Munich.

I believe that was how SAP pursued this and many other things, whether object orientation or distributed data banks. Let the others first cut their teeth on bringing new technologies past the laboratory stage; that is not the job of SAP. Nonetheless, the impression still persists that the development of the R/3 applications system actually was motivated from basic development.

Freedom for a new applications paradigm

PLATTNER At this time (the end of the 1980s), we also thought that with the R/2 system we had reached such a high degree of functionality for business administration software that from then on, we only had to deal with a change in technology. We did not think at all in the first years of the R/3 project about keeping our eyes open for a paradigm shift in the applications design. So we again built a system for the professional user in the specialized departments of a business—for accounting, for the production control department, for purchasing.

Now we have a business administration system with the R/3. At the beginning of the 1990s, it had something like the functionality of the R/2 system, but with an entirely different architecture—not on the mainframe computer, which was quite the style at the time, and widely scaleable from very small to very large, but with the same business administration orientation. This scaleable nature and the reduced cost of the computers opened up a new dimension, namely the dimension of better meeting the needs of the user. We had to think about who our user is—not just the specialist in the technical departments, but also the occasional user.

The result was that we had to put a lot more into the applications programming and structure the applications with more trade-offs to comply with the user's needs. Throughout the 70s and 80s, we put limited effort into meeting the user's needs. We always told the user, "That's nice, what you would like to have, but you can only get so much out of a computer. And you will have to get used to that. You will just have to learn to get along with the system." That is what the mainframe world, the central data processing world, exuded in arrogance toward the user.

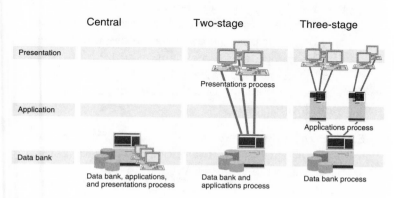

The client/server architecture of the R/3 system.

SCHEER The mainframe was expensive and barely paid for itself. The user was therefore supposed to learn how to make proper use of the expensive machines.

PLATTNER Through our principle—that is, the three-level client/server principle with the applications servers—we could provide, as compared with the R/2 mainframe system, the same user numbers at lower hardware costs with better performance. And as our system became technically better and the famous RISC workstations became faster and faster—first 50 MIPS, then 100 MIPS, and today the PC has 300 MIPS—what we delivered became cheaper and cheaper. We received this development as a gift of the times. Suddenly, we had computer capacity in excess. You no longer worry about the resource in short supply, but rather you can choose the cheapest resource.

The user at the center

This change in trends led us to approach the user in a different way. We think, "How can the system make the user's life easier? How can we reach new and different classes of users?" For example, managers who do not want to take a course to learn how to carry out a certain transaction. If they want to do more than just look at a couple of lists and want to perform an evaluation themselves, the system should support them in a way that they can learn while performing the act itself. New and comprehensive software is necessary for this. This only becomes possible once we remove the bottleneck of "The computer is too expensive and too slow" through our technology and hardware development and the combination of our architecture and the hardware development.

SCHEER This brings a new focus to development as well. Until now, the SAP software for business-wide applications was in the forefront. We had to make strategic decisions for SAP to act, such as, "We will set up the entire accounting system with SAP and come up with a new organization for the entire consolidation of our complicated business." Now we are taking another look at this business-wide, all-encompassing business view and going back to the individual workplace.

User-centered computing is the new catch phrase because in the final analysis, the acceptance of the individual employee decides the productivity of such a dispersed and highly integrated system.

PLATTNER The needs of the individual.

SCHEER When the employees in the background are still working with their old filing cabinets and just tinkering around on the keyboards of this fantastic system, then you have not achieved any efficiency.

PLATTNER We had been in the glass house too long. We failed to recognize that it is not enough when all the professional users of a specialized department use our system in their specialized functions. Even when all the employees of the personnel department can work perfectly with the system, they are still just a part of the employees in the business who have an interest in personnel data. It took a while before we recognized that we were making a system not just for the personnel department, but for the entire company. After all, who actually needs the information from the personnel department? The managers are responsible for personnel, not the personnel department.

Opening up to new classes of users

This shows the trend in America where the actual personnel department is shrinking drastically, and the classic personnel tasks are performed by the employees themselves, entering and maintaining their own basic information. That is a change in trends and, I believe, the right way to go. We only realized this at SAP once the number-one argument against the demands of the users, the limitations on expensive resources, disappeared.

SCHEER The trend in utilization of the system not only by subject specialists is continuing. We are not simply saying that personnel management is not exclusively the task of the personnel department and every manager is also a personnel manager; the same idea applies as well to the controller, for example. Controlling is not the task of the controlling department, but rather every manager and every employee is responsible for directing his activities at the goals of the business. Ideas such as self-controlling demonstrate this development. Then you have the desire to evaluate the efficiency of transactions at individual workplaces. In principle, this also applies to information management. It is true that every manager is also an information manager. The result is immensely expanded usage of business administration software.

The Internet

PLATTNER Now we get this marriage of what 15 years of personal computing has created. Namely, the enterprise system is wedded with tools that can make life easier for the individual user, let him manage things better for himself—retrieving and displaying data from all the areas that interest him in a personal format, in a relatively simple operation, without a lot of time spent in learning the system. This marriage of tools and system and the discovery of new classes of users—the entire management of a company, all the employees of the company, and beyond that the partners of a company right down to the end consumers—that is a new world of computing that has been enormously promoted through the Internet.

But the Internet is, after all, just technology. My statement quoted earlier, "We are doing it because we can do it" also applies here. Now we can bring the end consumer to an enterprise system—the 5,000 customers in the world can be connected to the central ERP system—and that is a great change. What gratifies me personally about this is that through our decision about the architecture in the 90s, the early 90s, in the R/3 system, we preserved this room to be creative, and it comes easy to us to carry out such applications paradigm shifts.

It always hurt me that until '94, that is, almost right up until today, our competition insisted that the R/3 system is just a ported R/2 system. But after all the discussion we have had here, it should be clear that nothing was taken from the R/2 and that the new system was constructed on a totally different computer concept. Not that many people can let you explain in a few minutes the fundamental differences between the R/3 architecture and the R/2 architecture. It has always bothered me to hear such talk because we worked very hard here to build a totally different system. Others who had never taken the trouble to look more closely into the R/3 have said it is just a ported R/2 system.

R/3 is not a ported R/2

WENDT The accusations of the competition can at best apply to the applications architecture. The applications paradigm of the R/3 system was not changed, but the technological architectural paradigm was radically changed and created the basis for a change in the applications paradigm.

A paradigm shift

SCHEER This was certainly true, because if the applications had been totally reconstructed, the new development would have been too complex.

WENDT You would have undoubtedly been overburdened by two such challenges. They can only be tackled sequentially, that is, resolved one after the other. You are constructing a new building, and first you have to put in the foundation for the new building; you cannot build the floors of the building at the same time. I mean that the technology that the R/3 incorporates had to be there first before you could consider a change in the applications paradigm.

This is a revolution, and practically everyone will have access to such a system over the Internet, without needing three weeks of training beforehand. And that will be great.

Chapter 3

Challenges for Software Development

It is therefore clear in the minds of most decision-makers that integrated business processes bring substantial advantages. And since it is technically possible, it is not far off that integrated business processes will be implemented across the boundaries of businesses. And now we are all thinking about specific solutions for this.

Walldorf, May 18, 1998

SCHEER Will the Internet be the driving force behind a new applications paradigm?

PLATTNER We are just at the beginning, but what is already becoming evident is that we will view business processes differently. We will develop them from the outside, from the customer viewpoint, and that naturally has an effect on the architecture of the applications. Applications will be more communications-centered or more user-centered. The user could be within the business or outside it, he could be a partner or the end consumer, and things that used to go through several levels of partners will now take a shortcut.

A new view of the business process

We already have such developments in the purchasing systems for non-production materials, where the user just orders them directly out of a catalog and the fulfillment of the order is no longer handled through the central procurement system; rather, it is informed of the order only relatively late in the process. This whole subject is covered by the term "front office." The operative perspective is "outside-in," rather than the traditional centralized concept of "inside-out" that has been promulgated for more than 25 years. The latter view originated from core internal processes. They were defined and the data was gathered for them. Now that is changing. Direct processes you once performed manually are now executed through the system, even by users who are not working in the usual specialized department, but rather have a totally different job somewhere else. These systems look different and naturally have an effect on the user systems overall.

One example where this first became evident is the personnel department, which is mainly concerned with taking care of the personnel information of the employees. It is on the verge of being abolished. The employees are taking care of their information themselves because most of the data is, after all, personal information. They are the only ones who can decide what data is correct and which information has changed. And with appropriate technical support—we call it employee self-service—they are put in the position of taking care of their own information. This removes the traditional division of labor where the employees fill out forms and the specialized department reads the forms and enters the data from the forms into the computer. This traditional chain of processes is being completely transformed.

The user as process owner

WENDT Yes. This is natural because the original source of the information is, after all, the employee. If he moves, he and no one else in the business knows that he has changed his address. Earlier, however, he had to submit this information. Now it makes no difference whether he or his secretary reports it and thus starts this chain of events so that somewhere it is registered on a centralized basis, or whether he does it right away with the technical system and simply handles the matter. One way or the other, it has to be him who reports it.

PLATTNER Now we can and must look for all possible ways to replace the forms being used, for example, order forms about a sales promotion in a specialty magazine that arrives at your home—such as a golfing magazine or an order catalog for horse lovers—where you can check off all the articles. The menu is prepared beforehand with three variations on each item, and when it's complete, you have an order. In the last 10 years, many companies have organized themselves along these lines.

Now comes the step where I can let the end consumer order directly over the Internet, and through this, I achieve a new quality—because now, for the first time, I can engage the end consumer in a dialogue and ask what he does, what he is looking for, or what he is interested in. I receive not only the end product of his operation with the catalog, the filled-in order form, but I can also see how he works with the catalog. This is a new quality, and the top companies have already made this an essential component of their strategy.

Dell, for example, in its sale of PCs over the Internet, with its configuration over the Internet—that is a new quality. I no longer have to go to my PC store and get advice in a conversation or fill out a form there, but I can gather the information myself. Because I know best about my own activities, I can determine the configuration from that. Such processes stemming from the customer are totally new. He starts the process, controls the process even over great distances, and thus becomes the owner of the process.

SCHEER Can't we say that we are just now properly understanding and adapting to the applications development paradigm of networking? Upon the arrival of the client/server systems, it was still too soon to begin immediately with propagating new applications architectures, because the conversion of tools into applications concepts takes a long time before something truly innovative develops.

The dissimilarity of technological thrusts

I believe that an interval of time occurs between hardware innovation, the software technology innovation, and the applications innovation. The applications innovation requires the longest time to assimilate the technology. But the time has now come. It is also striking that similar approaches have simultaneously appeared in numerous branches. In sales, one speaks of "efficient consumer response," that is, an idea that the customer picks up something at a supermarket and a bell rings with the producer, telling him that he has to replace something. Over the entire chain stretching from the consumer through the retail and wholesale stores, we have a direct correlation between the transaction "The customer selects" and the response to this, "It has to be replaced." At the same time, we speak in the industry about "supply chain management," and that means taking a look at where we find the source of a process and who initiates it. Here again, we consider the entire logistics chain, not just up to the direct customer, but also to the customer of the customer. And simultaneously up to the supplier of the supplier.

This means that we are going much further in our organizational way of looking at things, which is, first of all, the understanding of networking. This change would have occurred even without the Internet; perhaps it is not such a dramatic change with client/server and traditional networking. But the Internet now naturally gives the whole thing a tremendous leap in scale.

The first dimension: integrated business processes

PLATTNER We had already gone far in the internal networking of classic business processes with R/2. The breakthrough came with R/3, however, because we suddenly had a technical platform that could be significantly better scaled and would let us develop the business processes from the very small to the very large. With R/3, we could also take care of the larger businesses. The catch phrase "business process reengineering" had over many years led to reorganizing integrated business processes for improving the organization of the internal functioning in a company. It became clear that integrated business processes made it possible for a company to react more swiftly and to work better. So it is only a small step from that to say we now need to think further, beyond the boundaries of the business.

It does not matter whether you do this with conventional technology or not; you can do it both ways. The fact is, however, that we suddenly had a systems technology world whose elements could be combined to a much greater extent. The systems could communicate, at first only in a technical way. In addition, with the Internet we had a network that was available on a truly worldwide basis.

All this took place simultaneously. It is therefore clear in the minds of most of the decision-makers that integrated business processes bring some significant advantages. And since it is technically possible, it is not far off that integrated business processes will be implemented across the boundaries of businesses. And now we are all thinking about specific solutions for this.

SCHEER There was time for us to develop because the managers of the specialized departments, who earlier had always only thought in functions, had already been mollified by years of discussions about internal business processes. They had already internalized the integration thinking as well. To take the thinking beyond the business boundaries while considering the catch phrases for "globalization," and so on, is almost a necessary step that simply did not need further justification.

The question now is whether, now that we have the technical prerequisites of communication, we are able to make standards available on the applications side. This means, for example, that each partner in an ordering process will always immediately understand the same thing. Even when the bits might be compatible, the content is not. Maybe this is why technicians such as EDI with their EDIFACT so far have still not made the big breakthrough, namely because they have defined things only at the syntactic level. I do in fact know where I will find the item number in an EDIFACT sentence, but I do not know what it means, what article is hidden behind a certain number.

It is therefore important for the applications software that large market leaders develop to move along the de facto standardization of the content. This development is starting to take place as businesses like OMG begin to standardize content such as the field description of the inventory.

The second dimension: differing types of users

PLATTNER A second dimension comes into play here as well. The applications we want to line up in a chain of processes reaching beyond the company and beyond a specific person deal with a great variety of user types. In the golden days of the R/2 system, the users were a relatively homogenous group. Now, however, practically every employee is a potential player in this integrated process chain, with totally different training and totally different interests. This is true for the engineer in the construction department as well as the end consumer who we served one time and who we want to reach again in a market promotion. The most varied groups of persons are caught up in this process chain.

This is also a new experience for SAP—that we have different groups of persons to deal with and that we must build various user interfaces for these various groups of persons. We can no longer get by with a single general task-processing module prepared by the specialist task development worker. We have the task one time as a self-service task performed by a consumer on the Internet, then we have it for setting up a sales office for occupation, then we have it as a repair task for a broken piece of equipment, we have it as an internal production task, and so on.

We utilize the same structures not only in different technical fields, but also in various user groups with yet another dimension. We need the repair order once for its disposition and the statistics on maintenance, and then we need it for the repairman who has to perform a very specific task. We see clearly that we must represent the same repair order differently for various people. We have to present it to whatever person in terms that make it understandable for their activities and their idea of the world. For the repairman, the most important thing is making repairs and fixing things; the repair order is only the impetus for his activities.

This leads to the conclusion that out of the central system, we have to define variants on the object "task" that show different faces to the various users of this object in the execution of the process.

WENDT The idea of depth of usage can be helpful here. When a repairman spends only 5 percent of his work time with the information object "task" and does something quite different in the remaining 95 percent, then it makes no sense to send him off for three weeks of training so that he can learn how to operate the system. A person who does technical work on the orders and from morning to night does not do anything else—he is, by contrast, ready to learn the operation of a complex order system. It is just the same as when someone wants to make coffee once or, at most, how to operate a coffee machine, whereas a pilot learns for two years before he is allowed to fly. The differences in the readiness to learn are enormous.

PLATTNER Yes, and the problem is not just that it has to be developed in one system or in one family of systems and not to build an application for each user and for each object. You would drop dead trying to integrate these applications components in this case. We do not have any global norms for a task, for its definition or its conditions. We also cannot put one together from components. We are a long ways away from such a thing being conceivable at all, at least not by the people who are deep into development. Everyone knows that two software systems concerned with similar subjects can be virtually incompatible. They can have different conceptual structures, data structures, and coding procedures so that the system which can show a variety of faces to various users is probably more apt to succeed than one in which variants are put together each time.

We need new software technologies

SCHEER This means that we need new software technologies. When we talk about software variants, then naturally we turn to the idea of object orientation. Here you can construct subtypes through heritage, and commonalities are automatically carried over. This variant of construction offers a high degree of reusability of the software. And this brings up comparisons with other industries such as the automobile industry or the aircraft industry, where you are always dealing with variant problems and therefore have experience in how you should deal with them neatly, that is, with a low degree of redundancy.

Coordination with different users is another question. Users are, after all, organizational units. The requirements for a function's presentation will be different depending on whether we are looking at a specialist, such as an engineer, or a consumer who is using the system in his home. Assigning functions to organizational units will therefore be the decisive factor. That means that when a function is assigned to an engineering department, I automatically have to show it differently than when it is assigned to a salesman's department, to marketing, or to outside services. Such variability in the software is already possible from a technical standpoint, in which such assignments are described through connections from organization and function models that define the corresponding variants.

But how do software publishers suddenly discover this diversity in customers? Earlier you only dealt with the EDP supervisor because you knew he was in charge of the budget, and now you have to think about so many different customer groups. How does a software publisher adapt to this situation?

PLATTNER Well, first of all, it was not only the EDP supervisor we dealt with because the specialized departments were always there; now it is just that the number and scope of the departments that you have to deal with are significantly greater.

Goodbye to the freedom from redundancy

On the other hand, we have a great advantage. In the first years, we said integration presupposes that we will build systems free of redundancy. We have data free of redundancy, everyone knows these data, and we can set up the transactions and chains of processes upon this pool of redundancy-free data. We stayed with this idea for quite a long time and made it one of the main distinguishing features of our systems.

Now it turns out that this flexibility in serving various groups of users almost inexorably leads to giving up this axiom of data storage free of redundancy and to allowing replicated data throughout.

Data bank producers came to this conclusion considerably earlier. We needed the influence of the object-oriented systems, I believe, this connection between program logic and data which shows that components are talking to components; it's not a mechanical data bank system distributing the data everywhere. Today we have gained a degree of freedom in which we store redundant data in a somewhat different form and automatically maintain it so that we can build an application for other groups of addressees from it.

The simplest example is a data warehouse in which, on one hand, we have the operating system for the transactions and, on the other hand, a system for evaluation and planning, a so-called decision support system application, a new data bank. But we are now seeing this in other systems as well, whether it is the Advanced Planner and Optimizer (APO) system or the Sales Force

Making new applications possible through redundancy of data

Automation (SFA) system. They all first and foremost have a redundant data inventory organized in a different form from the data inventory for the operational applications. The data organization in each case pursues different goals. When, for example, a simulation application is not fast enough, it rapidly loses any significance. If I cannot produce a configuration simulation in a couple of seconds, then the salesman cannot use it in an online conversation. The efficiency of the applications relies upon redundant data, among other things.

When the salesman cannot take the relevant data for his group of customers with him on a laptop so that he will have it available on an airplane or while he is sitting around in a waiting room somewhere, then there is really no application. It is not a practical suggestion for him at that point to retrieve the data from the central repository over a modem and a telephone line.

We fought against this data redundancy for quite a long time and demanded that data processing take place online, that is, in real time—that you had to go into the system. Now data can be encapsulated and maintained in another system. We have solved the problem of synchronization, and suddenly new applications can be built with this redundant data. This is a very important feature. Almost all the new applications we are building and addressing to totally new groups of users have their own data, which is often redundant.

WENDT I often remark on the following two aspects when I lecture on freedom from redundancy. Once we sought freedom from redundancy at the input stage. In your everyday life, you do not want to enter the same information over and over after you have already provided it once—for example, address and telephone number when you are filling out a form—although copying within a system was never particularly expensive.

Basically, every buffering of more than two milliseconds is a loss of freedom from redundancy. We then have the data on the disk and again in the working memory. It is more a question of whether I know that I have copied it. Let us take, for example, a textbook. Many people have the same book at the same time. Regarding the memory storage, this is guaranteed not to be free of redundancy, but that is totally unimportant because the textbook remains stable over a longer period of time. And critical data that change every two milliseconds cannot be accessed by someone on an airplane with his laptop, but in most cases, that does not matter.

SCHEER The basic problem of data redundancy is the update, and we have seen that simple procedures have proven themselves among the various possible procedures. These are centralized procedures; that is, you allow decentralized copies of the centralized data, but the update of these copies occurs through the central data. You avoid an update over a "two-phase commit" protocol, for example.

PLATTNER There is some truth in that. The subject of decentralized and centralized is quite complicated. Decentralized is faster and more flexible and can adjust more rapidly, but through its diversity, decentralization bears the seeds of chaos and higher costs. In our context, this means at first there was a lot developed on a decentralized basis, as individual components, and then popped into a process somewhere with its own data. Later, however, when these processes are stabilized, the components can again be integrated into the central system.

The difference between "centralized" and "decentralized" must be reconsidered

We are already experiencing this now with Internet applications that tend to be centralized, now that this is no longer unfamiliar territory and the technology has been mastered. The same holds true for new programming languages on the design of images. Once the technology is mastered, there is much to be said for integrating things into a centralized system. The costs for operating the system are less in a centralized system, the security is higher, and the coordination is easier.

With process chains that include the entire operation, more systems are beginning to build a process chain. Some of these process chains tend to be captured by centralized systems that are not necessarily the systems of the producing businesses. They can now also be service systems, such as worldwide reservations systems or other broker systems, that are no longer anonymous systems behind an airline's counter, but also are available to other systems.

The comprehensive business integration movement

We are now at the point of bringing our business process chains into these systems or connecting the systems into our business processes. What I see before us is a system with many worldwide net nodes that dovetail with each other in varying degrees. The interconnection is naturally stronger within a business than between businesses, but the systems no longer have definite boundaries; rather, an interweaving of the systems within and outside a business will go much further.

Earlier a library had precisely the content determined by its inventory of books. Today, in contrast, every library has an Internet window and can display all books that are for sale or another electronic library. Once the entry into a system is digitized, other digital systems can access it. This is another source that is driving the integration movement beyond systems tied to the business.

A key experience: repairs on an ocean-going yacht

I had a key experience six weeks ago when my skipper on the ocean-going yacht *Morning Glory* climbed up on the mast with a camera, took pictures of the pulleys where the halyards come out from the mast top, climbed back down, and came down on the bosun's chair. He sat down at a PC on the boat, loaded the picture from the digital camera, and then sent the picture over the boat's telephone connection to the mast builder in Illinois, near Detroit, Michigan. Barely an hour later, he received an answer about how the mast builder's engineer thought a problem could be fixed.

Just a short while ago, we could not have imagined this whole process.

Before, someone would have had to climb up, take a photo, and then take the photo to be developed. This would have disrupted the process right there, because my skipper would have had to return to America two days later. However, within two hours we made a decision about specific changes to a part of the structure. And this was not a matter of connecting Boeing and Lufthansa, but rather units. So you can use such a technology even when it does not involve a lot of people. How much will be possible tomorrow when the normal end consumer will be able to communicate with his "business partners," that is, with the suppliers?

Just think what it costs when a service technician arrives and takes a look at something. It takes a while before he recognizes the problem after he has taken a look at it; then he repairs it and leaves. Lay out this whole chain in a diagram and think about what it costs to make the plans; he also has to be able to do the work, so training costs enter into it. He traveled, then he looked at the problem, and then he drove back, and finally the EDP writes a bill for this. Why do we wonder why repairs cost so much by the hour?

If you think about it, the digital camera is now a standard. You take a picture of the problem, and the manufacturer has it a short while later over an Internet connection. Process chains like this were not conceivable only a short time ago, and I am sure that in the near future we can expect many such devices to be available at affordable prices. We are familiar with this process from our own programs; it is very hard to give a purely verbal description of content.

Digitalization opens new possibilities

Two people who are not used to talking with each other will not have the same idea about what they are seeing on a screen; it is a very difficult matter. In our example, two totally different media can communicate with each other. Scanning in photos, a bit of technology, is suddenly available, and I can send a photo as an attachment to mail and accomplish the process in a totally different way.

SCHEER We are now talking a lot more about applications examples and discussing this from a use orientation. After the technology is available and understood, it is just these aspects of using applications that drive the next wave of development. It is no longer enough to say that R/3 is good because it is based on client/server technology; now you have to describe cases where you can build neat process chains upon it with a high use potential.

It is not the technology but the application that counts

PLATTNER Yes, it is quite clear that unlike 10 or 15 years ago, it does not matter that you have mastered a CICS application, but we can now concentrate on the application, and it is simply of no interest what technology is involved. I say this even though we rode for quite a while on such technology waves. No one is interested any longer in the catch phrases, whether it is object orientation or component technology. It is enabling technology.

The truly interesting and exciting thing is what we now can do. We no longer need to describe why we are employing a technology because that interests only the engineer. He knows why you need components and how the components reside on the various systems and communicate thanks to COM or CORBA integration. But the exciting thing is what applications are possible now.

SCHEER Earlier, certain technical concepts were "killer arguments." If you asked a software producer, "Do you have a relational data bank in your system?" and he answered, "No," then you would choose another system. Or later, client/server technology was a deal breaker. I believe that these technical arguments will no longer have this significance. If you ask, "Do you have object orientation?" and the answer is "No," this issue is no longer a deal breaker today.

WENDT That is also right. After all, the driver is not interested in how the engineer built the engine. There is indeed such an oddity as a car with 16 cylinders and the camshaft on top, but this is an exception.

PLATTNER (Laughs) My car must have two camshafts on top and aluminum cylinder heads.

SCHEER Can we get back to the question of communications standards? SAP made a great contribution here through its market power. For me, I notice this when two people talk and use the concept of "accounting district" [Buchungskreis]; I know they are both using SAP. That means certain SAP language constructs have simply taken hold, such as "works" [Werk] in an SAP context. Even the banks are talking about works because they need this concept definition for configuration or they are talking about production groups.

Communications standards

PLATTNER We are in the process of changing this to fit the concepts closer to the language of the branches.

SCHEER Yes, that is changing. But I only wanted to show what a significant impact has already been achieved and that we must continue to create norms for the content as well.

WENDT Aren't you being very optimistic? When Mr. Plattner was talking about the mast photo, you have to keep in mind that the story was entirely free of semantics. The skipper understood the picture; it is just characters being transmitted, and the recipient gets the picture. That is simple. By way of contrast, I consider it very difficult to build a semantically determined interface where what is being sent from one end is interpreted by the system at the other end and reproduced with the same syntax. Just as we are now speaking German with each other, and what comes out of my mouth is not detected by your ear as simply variations in air pressure but is

Boundaries of standardization

recognized as the German language. If you have no command of the German language, then the arrangement does not work.

SCHEER But even with commercial applications, you can surely standardize more than is the case at the moment. I cannot entirely determine whether it is as feasible with the content as it is with the technology, but I also do not see why each business has to put together its own invoice, develop its own article description, and create its own personnel data description. There are certainly some things you can define in a general way.

PLATTNER That was the reason for standard software, and these things have become standardized. Now we can see whether we can go further.

SCHEER This standardizing through the software has only been achieved through the market power of the key player. Earlier, when there were still 150 PPS systems in Germany, there were also 150 different inventory definitions and work plan definitions.

WENDT It was just the same with the screws until the threading was standardized. You have to recognize first the advantage of standardization and realize that one is not better than the other, it is just different, and therefore it makes sense for us to agree on a single solution.

The new digital world

PLATTNER It is certainly an important matter to standardize the typical data objects that are exchanged between various systems and various producers or between systems of the same producer. But I want to bring up the example of the photo from the mast top once more. It shows that it is suddenly possible for us to connect very different things. So the entire world of office operations—the correspondence, the filing, the faxes—should all be digitized. Everything that can be digitized is available for our classic transactional data processing.

After we considered multimedia to be our own realm for a long time, we are doing integration over various presentation forms. Where, up until now, we have dealt only with formatted data with a little text, now the attachment—such as a pixel picture—is a significant form of information. Now it comes about that we must describe and store the attributes of this picture in a classic form, because we cannot take these attributes directly from the image. You have to store them separately, because of tolerances and such. We put the descriptive information together with the illustration, and the costs of multimedia are controllable through compression technology. Suddenly it is also possible to send and store moving images at a low cost, as well as relate it to formatted information. Meanwhile, we are moving further to where speech input, speech output, and even gestures can also be incorporated in computer systems.

There is almost always a fundamental change when something is available on the PC. The high-tech realm has had multimedia for a long time now. How long have we already been doing professional graphic data processing? How long have we already been doing speech input and speech output, at least in the laboratory? But only when these technologies were available on the PC did their expansion explode. The PC as a crystallization seed is therefore very important for new applications scenarios and new applications technologies. This massive availability of a technology— whether it is digitized pictures or highly compressed moving images or speech input or output systems—is what is important. At the moment they are available on the PC, you can build standard systems.

The PC as a crystallization seed

The 15 years of development in office applications also demonstrates this. At first, the applications were isolated PC systems, then they were integrated because you used them in the office environment in an integrated manner, and for five years now, they have also had quite an influence on professional systems in specialized departments and must be connected with them. They now are coming over the PC into our enterprise systems.

SCHEER It was not any different with the Internet. The American parents used it to exchange email with their kids at college. And then a lawyer knew how to work with a PC, at least how to write email, and subsequently he also began to use it in his office.

Will SAP become a producer for consumers?

Does this not mean that a software publisher such as SAP will now also become a producer of consumer goods? We have already cited this example from Andy Grove about the so-called inflection point. There was an inflection point for Intel when the error in the Intel mathematics processor showed up. It was a rounding-off error that surfaced in very few cases. Suddenly, however, this error that they knew about at Intel and were going to fix in the next release was on the front page of *USA Today*. You saw how this business became a consumer producer all at once. Thousands of consumers called to find out what was up with their PCs and whether they could use them any more. Intel had never delivered anything to a single consumer, but rather had supplied IBM and other manufacturers, not Mr. Jones or Mr. Smith. But suddenly it had become a de facto consumer producer.

It cost more than 100 million dollars to settle this matter. The problem was not fixing the technical error, but repairing the image and positioning themselves anew. I therefore believe that a software publisher that until now had the EDP supervisor and the technical department chief as customers and suddenly is dealing with the end customers (in much the same way that the employee and not the personnel department now operates the personnel system) must present itself in a different way.

PLATTNER That is another quality, doubtless, and also another risk domain. I see it in exactly the same way, but now it cannot be stopped. You can in fact say that we will not do any such thing, we will do something else, and we will handle only the back office processes. But we do not want to take this attitude because the share of the front office in the total system will clearly increase.

SCHEER That is also good. I only want to ask how a software business should change in order to address this new dimension, this exponentially increasing number of customers.

PLATTNER There must be significantly more invested in observing the end user. It must be oriented toward the actual end user, toward the one who works with the system—and not just toward some theoretical user you imagine so that where there is no such user, you can bend the real user accordingly through training. At the contact interface, the system must be practically free of training and you must be able to operate it as naturally as you would a radio, where you learned just one time that you can dial in the station with this knob and make it louder or quieter with the other one. It is unimportant whether this functions only digitally or with a tuning knob. We learn in a matter of seconds how to operate a new radio. We must build our transactions in exactly the same way.

More end user research

Other branches that build equipment for end users put in a lot of this end-user research. And we have an advantage with our software. We can actually react rapidly; we can change the face of software very quickly and modify it very quickly because there is no mechanical production involved. We can also see very quickly how our product looks to others, but it is certainly an area where we must invest an order of magnitude more.

The good thing is that the closer we come to the source of the interaction, the more the spectrum of functionality narrows down. We do not have to make available the entire business administration of the SAP systems. Rather it is truly a small extract for a class of user. The important thing is to work out what these extracts include. This is not easy because the world is changing greatly, and the whole system is just now being created. You have to set it up so that you can reach the greatest possible number of users without any complaints.

Reduction in complexity

WENDT That example with the radio, the semantic network there is very small. What concepts do you have to learn if you still don't know at all what a radio is and you want to operate it? You have to know that it can be turned on and off, you have to know that it has an acoustic source that you can select, and then you can make it louder or softer and that is all. By way of contrast, the semantic network for business administration applications is significantly more complex. If someone is sitting in front of a purchase or sales form, for example, he has to master many possibilities for input and output. It will certainly be a considerable task to break down this complexity into parts and modularize it so that it can be easily learned from a semantic standpoint and intuitively comprehended.

PLATTNER In one of our developmental departments, we are involved with applications in the hotel field. The idea is to expand the R/3 system with new process chains that extend from the R/3 into other systems. Then you cannot operate our classic purchase form for the chef or sous-chef. The entire purchase must be controlled through touch-screen applications and through menus of 500 positions that will be ordered over and over in a kitchen by clicking on the product from the catalog and giving the quantity you want to order and perhaps also the delivery schedule. The transaction "purchase" is thus simplified to the absolute minimum, and you don't have to enter the company or location because it is established since the installation. You must consider all possible system parameters individually as to whether you need them for this application in the kitchen.

We tested this in practical use. It was not clear at the beginning whether we would have to write new parts for the ordering system. The experiment showed, however, that we did not have to write anything new. We can operate a totally normal R/3 ordering system through the new interaction we offer to the system, and it will buy the strawberries and the fresh asparagus and everything else you need in a good kitchen. But we have, moreover, the conveniences of the powerful transaction processing R/3 system, that it can pull things together, that it provides statistical information on the purchasing procedures, that it can post the delivery dates, and so on. These functions can then be processed by the purchasing department—there is also one in a hotel—in order to grasp not the operational but the financial side of purchasing, such as calculating the costs, support for writing contracts, and so on. Coming out of heavy industry, we have developed our systems for all those things.

We can point out more and more possibilities, build special transactions channels for groups of users, or implement other technologies such as touch screen. In doing this, the learning process should approach zero because you will be able to operate the system intuitively. It must be simplified so that the semantic network is so negligible you immediately grasp it.

What we perfectionists cannot underestimate is the developmental costs. These "simple" functions are to be made available to multiple accounting circles simultaneously, in multiple languages, and run simultaneously in multiple currencies . . . well, I could go on for hours like this, the way a typical SAP developer thinks.

But it will go in this direction because we have, on the one hand, back-end engines—and not just one, but many—that are quite complex, and you greatly simplify this complexity for certain groups of users. This leads, however, to redundant transactions, and you have to duplicate the business processes in part. We do not have only one generic solution with a couple of special functions, but rather we have many various processing variants at the front end. But we are already quite a ways down this path. Telephone sales must take place differently from the initial installation of a drug store or a pharmacy. They are simply something different, even though both are task processing.

This demands more observation of the user and also much discussion with the back end so that the front and back ends do not go their own separate ways. SAP is faced with this problem on a very large scale. We maintain variations for various classes of users, we maintain variations for various industries, and we maintain variations for many other subsystems, for other technologies, that are embedded within.

SCHEER But this also means that the SAP developer in back office must continue to master the high level of complexity. He must also think in terms of complicated alternatives in order to ward off, to a certain degree, the possibility of errors that could be passed on to the front office. On the other hand, he naturally cannot shift all the requirements to the front office and say, "I want just one correct task set and I won't accept anything else," but rather he must behave in a way that tolerates errors. He must also deal with fuzzy information and accept it. We must make sure that the back office systems do not again destroy this soft interface with the front office later.

PLATTNER That really is a danger. I sometimes use the expression "task processing." If you set up the general transaction, which can do everything and is accordingly complicated, in many simple variations, what does this mean for the modification services? We have always had a real fear about this, a panic attack. Now it is probable that a change we make somewhere in a central component will not penetrate into all the other variants we have previously built. But this is new territory.

An alternative is also that the various systems handle various aspects and were developed by various people and then later coupled together. Then you have to agree on a relatively soft coupling.

WENDT Yes, that can become a problem because then the integration does not work any more.

PLATTNER The reverse difficulty that can come up for us is related to our experience. We know what diversity we can offer, so every single simplification appears artificial to us. We always ask ourselves, "Have we also thought about this situation; how will you handle each exception?" But if we say instead, "We will make the radio so simple, we will make purchasing by picking from a list so simple, that we will not allow any special situations to come up," then we are making a decision that under certain conditions we might later have to retract.

WENDT Yes, but is it so bad when we have to retract it later? When it is relatively so easy to build a second radio?

PLATTNER Yes. But we have always been terrified by this, although a company like Sony has actually shown us the way. When you look in the Sony catalog, a lot of equipment that is not very different from each other is actually going after the same market. They have a different name and show a different face, the detailed description list points out the differences, and we actually do not know how much they might have in common. The Sony company and others in this branch are not at all afraid to build a new item of equipment. But we are panicked at the thought of building another new transaction on the same subject.

No fear of variants

We have always had this fear and—another glance into the past—it got into our heads at SAP when we brought R/1 to the IMS in the form of R/1.5. We had built a task processing system at ICI as a forerunner of the SAP systems, and it had painted different pictures for each different type of task, such as an urgent task or a follow-up to an existing task, an initial task, and so on. Today you could say that it depicted various transactions. And then we tried to find the least common denominator and to program this commonality.

We had a lot of variants in the beginning, but we already had a purchasing system, an accounting system, and a rudimentary sales system. When we sold all these systems to the Freudenberg Company, the IMS system people told us that we were not allowed to have more than 256 forms in an application that ran in one address space. R/3 today has approximately 25,000. We therefore had to restrict ourselves and channel everything over the same forms. The IMSers had thought that applications are actually independent of each other, and each partial application then has 256 screens so that would just have to do. But we wanted to integrate our applications.

Many SAPers in leadership jobs today came to SAP at this time, the beginning of the 80s. This experience left its mark on all of us; it left its mark on the entire R/2 that the number of screens had to be limited. Variants are evil things. Instead of saying, "What is so bad about variants? I'm simply building a new radio." Perhaps I just need to build a new front end and otherwise take the usual radio, and the rest is marketing. So this is an important process taking place with us today, one that must take place, where we recognize variants and do not get such a complex over a simple variant that is not so far from the generic.

New software architectures

SCHEER With that, we are in principle already getting into new software architectures. What comes through here is a form of broker architecture, where there is a decentralized system on one hand that must also be centrally controlled on the other hand.

PLATTNER It is going in this direction. We want to define a provisional standardized interface with our BAPIs, the Business APIs, that we can keep constant over the releases so that you can depend on it with your applications being modified. We started this three years ago and are pushing the development strongly, particularly where SAP partners are building further on extending the process chains or can couple their applications with those of SAP.

Another methodology has already proven itself to be relatively stable, and it can be rapidly implemented. I am thinking here about ITS, the Internet Transaction Server—namely that the front end of the application will be implemented, for example, on a Web server with HTML or Java applets. Then the interaction will take place in a special ABAP applications program, and through this the front end talks to all others in an ABAP applications program. Now if that goes through a standard BAPI interface, then we have a stable and elegant solution.

We have pursued these approaches in the new system for hotel applications as well. We wrote the front ends, the touch-screen front ends, in Java for simplified applications. The Java program shares its results with the ABAP interaction program that for its part is being driven by SAP R/3 transactions. And the advantage is that we can rapidly drive other ABAP programs with ABAP. In the communications from ABAP to ABAP, we have accomplished a number of things, similar to what the Java concept propagates, that make program-to-program integration possible. With this, we can rapidly build such variants, just as with radios, without any overly complicated interface definitions.

Basically we need a repository of interfaces. I build the interfaces so that they are universal interfaces, and

The universal interface and integration of technologies

the integration of technology is not affected by releases. Then the standardization problems come right at us. This takes its own time. In addition, we must support the integration of various technologies in as simple a way as possible. Java makes it possible to execute the interaction in an environment constructed in any manner, but a light environment; by light environment, I mean that I do not need a large PC for it. I go from this Java environment into our ABAP language, right on the applications server of the R/3 system, and then drive the R/3 system. With this we can rapidly build secure transactions, and we can think later about a universal interface.

I am not sure whether the ordering example from the hotel industry is really such a general case that we can deduce correctly from that system for all possible products, that is, PCs, productions material, and so on. Taken just in and of itself, it is a good solution. There is always the path of building the perfect universal interface, but we need a lot of time to do that.

SCHEER Concepts such as soft coupling, error-tolerant communications exchange, no standards—does this horrify the information technician, or is this exactly the direction in which software or applications architectures are imagined by the information technician? Where you actually deal more with concepts such as correctness verification by software, hard things, and where you do not call software engineering a science, but really just say it is something soft that we cannot explain through science.

The radio illustration

PLATTNER I don't know if it fits, but we have brought in the image of radio. . . . Now I have the front panels of electronic instruments in my mind's eye, how we arrange the individual elements of the front panel and to what degree the operation is mechanical or movement sensitive, whether you are turning a knob or perhaps changing it through a digital submodule. For the end user, it is entirely inconsequential if this knob architecture—let this be the example for a front-end architecture—is carried over into the core module of the system that lies behind it. Whether the transformation from front-end module into the logic of the radio, whether this is a component part of the radio, whether it is an element in between, or whether the component is mechanical in nature with a bit of electronics—that actually does not matter. What I want to say in this illustration is—let us now look at the radio module development technology that lies behind this—that we can rapidly tie in with various switching technologies and interface technologies; this is perhaps a development of the past year.

When we take a look at the development of ABAP and of Java, there are a lot of parallels. ABAP anticipated things in 1991, when it started to run in the client/server environment, that today are among the core elements of Java: how, by itself, it distributes itself to computers on the Net; that it compiles on its own, on the fly, when it is changed; that it rests upon a central repository, and so on. There are many relationships and therefore Java and ABAP understand each other very well. This is an important point: Programming languages are not as egocentric as they were 20 years ago, such as PL1 and COBOL. You could get them to work together only through very formal, clumsy interfaces.

ABAP and Java

The connection of various development systems has become much better. We can build in the functionality of Java and front-end systems simply and cheaply; perhaps this is not the best and most elegant way in which to build, but it is very cost effective. We can rapidly convert this functionality in a world where we have a lot of experience and a lot of people with a command of this world. We have distribution logistics so that we can use the existing modules we have in the middle layer very easily to build variants.

We have thought about alternatives in which we can make this route more systematic, and we have done proper development projects that have all led to very complicated structures. I will not rule out that in the future things might develop in this direction—with formal description about which object is actually being dealt with, who is concerning themselves with it, and what kind of hierarchy there is for partial views of this object. When you try to get a grip on this in a formal manner, you can easily build a very large broker system, but possibly miss the target, namely to build 500 front-end variants for the existing transactions.

These variants, consisting of a front panel and modules behind it, are of a different sort than "I want to connect this piece of equipment with another piece of equipment." There is a different quality to making a connection from a radio to an amplifier, to a recording system, or to a television system than putting a new front panel on a piece of equipment—only because we have always said that now we have new user groups. It is partly enough that we simply put various front-end operations panels on the same existing modules. Then when the programs communicate with each other, we must employ carefully built interfaces because programs are very sensitive when the interfaces change. So I have to construct these interfaces much more carefully.

SCHEER Which makes the interfaces in a salesman's system or logistics system more complicated than that between pieces of entertainment electronics equipment.

PLATTNER Significantly more complicated. If you are negligible in your definition of an interface, it will not get used and you can go ahead and build another new one. That is the big problem with interfaces. What can you leave out so that the interface does not become overly complicated? Interfaces can easily become too complicated.

The semantic determination of interfaces

WENDT You asked before whether the so-called soft interfaces are based on some tradition of software production, information science, or a self-evident rule of information science. When you are talking about interfaces, you always have to ask what the interface provides from a functional standpoint. The question of the functionality is independent of the question of how the relationships of the building blocks will be implemented from a software technology standpoint.

In the meantime, we have learned to keep the two questions separated from each other in dealing with hardware interfaces. Think, for example, about a bus, a hardware bus, which has slots where you can mount the boards for electronic components. The specifications for such a bus stipulate only the communications protocol, but not the semantics of the information content being exchanged. Such a bus is suitable for the communication of an extremely broad range of equipment that differs in capacity. Then a very powerful, error-tolerant, flexible, and adaptive piece of equipment, one that is capable of learning, can be right next to a very primitive piece of equipment. The equipment functionality does not go into the description of the interface, and those interfaces are particularly good when you can subsequently bring into play a large functional diversity, which you could not even consider in writing the interface specifications.

You cannot restrict the specifications of the interfaces to the communications semantics that occur to you when you let your imagination go free. It is guaranteed that a little later you will think of communications content that you left out. With a good interface, you very generally determine that there are function call-ups without determining what kind of functions they are. You have to plan that parameters for the function call-ups must be delivered along with them, so you deliberately leave the number of parameters open. When you specify such an interface, you have said nothing about the semantics of the function and its parameters, but rather you have utilized the semantics for the two words "function" and "parameter" that come from mathematics. By way of example, the CORBA system provides distributed objects to that type of interface for communications. The semantics of the functions called up did not go into the specifications of CORBA. Interfaces of that type have a long life span. You can comfortably base large systems on such interfaces. If, by contrast, you build the semantic stipulations into the interfaces, you can predict that something will soon occur to you where you will say, "Now I actually need this or that in addition," but it will no longer be possible.

This same thing applies to language as well, that is, for the design of programming languages and specifications languages. The semantics of such languages must be very generic. You can only bring in abstract so-called meta-concepts and you cannot be specific. For example, a programming language recognizes only a few data types from which you can put together whatever other data types you want; that is, the programming language is based on an ability to be expanded to whatever degree desired.

I am convinced that a good software architect must always keep his eye on the need to keep the semantic diversity separate from the protocol that carries it. If he does not do this, he builds a bad interface or a bad carrier system. This is true also for a system of the type about which you were just speaking, one that contains an adaptive core capable of learning, which can provide all possible small, special peripheral processes. The adaptability of the core, which consists of the core being able to handle surprising peripheral behavior that was not planned, cannot be housed in the interface, but rather must be executed as a functional expansion inside the core.

BAPIs   **PLATTNER** I see what has been said all the time in the background of our BAPIs. We indeed have diversity in various business administration functions—and there is an almost infinite diversity—and we have to define the semantic content of the individual BAPI interfaces. Everything you have said hits the nail right on the head; at the moment you set down the stipulations, you already know that there will be changes and that you will somehow have to deal with the incompatibility.

To call for establishing norms, that helps a bit perhaps. EDI has naturally helped a great deal because the more businesses talk to each other electronically, the more it will come out that you do not want to keep defining certain things anew, but rather expect that your partner has this type of interface. The most primitive would be, for example, that I can store an address with the assumption that the other person will understand it is an address so that he can continue with it. Some of these things have already had norms set and are being utilized more and more.

SCHEER Whereby it is also important to use such an EDI interface internally for one's own system development, even if you will not be exchanging data externally, because if you have a standard, you can easily use it for the data structure instead of thinking it over again. Despite the generic interface, there must always be a precise arrangement with data exchange; that is, conversion procedures must be set by the recipient or the sender.

PLATTNER Today when we put together an interface and couple two systems, we must always take care that the output A is a suitable interface for the application B on the input side. With all the applications we are now coupling, the situation almost always comes up that even when the other person is thinking in BAPIs on the output side, these BAPIs are not compatible with our SAP input BAPIs, so we need a bit of software in between.

WENDT This is not a matter of software, which can be of a generic nature. Here the person, the program developer, must make the semantic adjustments.

PLATTNER Yes.

SCHEER If you were to make the BAPIs even more generic now, the individual expense would become even greater. When the BAPIs are semantically relatively high and the sender knows the specifications and sticks to them. . . .

PLATTNER Yes, then the costs are reduced.

SCHEER And when he is not aware of them, naturally he gets some kind of garbage.

The fear of the system producer

PLATTNER That is the movement now. That is why companies that are developing interface technology are sprouting up all over the world. They connect two systems, even if they do not understand much about the systems themselves. That is the psychological problem of the system producer. System producer A and system producer B both have a terrible fear of working on the connection of their systems because they also have other partners, and they are afraid that if they do it with one, they will have to do it with the others as well.

The n:m relationship is a problem in software development. On the one hand, we want competition and there are more ERP offers and more front-end offers, and now every front-end supplier must be able to work with every ERP supplier and vice versa.

On proper and false analogies

SCHEER Now we are getting into a very complex problem area, that of heterogeneous software that we want to connect with simultaneously integrated processes developed over them. One likes to work with illustrations and analogies here. We also did that previously. Because we have trouble explaining the software, we used the radio as an example. Such analogies help, but sometimes they also lead us into error. When we want to connect the receiver with the loudspeakers and the tape deck as well, a simple solution is easy to come by, and you just get some compatible plugs.

PLATTNER In the analogue world, it is relatively simple, but it is somewhat more difficult in the digital world.

SCHEER A radio only has a few jacks, so I know where I can plug in the loudspeakers. But in the applications software, the connections are worlds more complicated. The example that fit alright in looking at the connections for the front end does not fit so well for the connection of the components.

PLATTNER Now we are building components in object-oriented technology where the components are easily expandable, and these components should be relatively simple to connect through a universal interface architecture. We can rapidly program components in a suitable programming language, and we can also rapidly define the interface architecture. Despite this, however, we have not yet succeeded in making individual components talk to each other because the complexity of the semantic exchange objects is too high.

SCHEER Let us stick with this for a while. It is wrong to say that we can build software we can stick together as we can the loudspeakers with the receiver in entertainment electronics. It is wrong to say that we can build software we stick together as components out of the Lego box because the illustrations are not the right ones. Lego building blocks have no content; they are just forms, each one like the next, whereas modules in the applications software are determined by their semantics and their syntax.

Components are not Lego building blocks

PLATTNER So the idea of Lego building blocks certainly does not fit here. A modern digital audio/video system is a degree higher than that. There we have data flows that must be converted until we get a picture or a sound. Without knowledge of the protocols, this conversion cannot happen. We can study the problems involved, but we must consider in doing so that our business administration interface problems are two or three orders of magnitude more complicated.

WENDT I would like to point out the differences between the two scenarios here. One is a component approach within a large company where they naturally have an internal standard established and thus can flexibly assembly their system by putting their components together. The other is a system manufacturer who declares, "Our modules are compatible with the modules from the competition." The second case is certainly more difficult to achieve than the first one. Let us take another look at the field of audio equipment. There we certainly find an internal standard so that everything a company produces—loudspeakers, amplifiers, tuners, and other things—fit together wonderfully. Even the newest loudspeaker model includes the appropriate plug, the one that has always been used.

But there is a problem when someone shows up with a radio from the competition because then the plug doesn't fit any more. It is therefore a lot easier for a company when there are internal standards for plugs, and the components do not have to be soldered together individually.

SCHEER I don't think that anyone would dispute that. However, we are not finished with where the illustrations fit and where they no longer fit. Sometimes you can be led into error by analogies that fit only partially. You constantly find the false image of Lego building blocks in literature. But where do we find examples that do fit well and from which we can also learn something to help us with our problems? Let us get into the realm of more complex systems, and take as an example the automobile industry.

Analogy: aircraft production and software engineering

PLATTNER Or, better yet, the aircraft industry.

SCHEER Yes, I want to get to this level of complexity. There we find cooperative working forms between the various partners, the component producers, and the assembler. There are concepts like simultaneous engineering, concurrent engineering, and so on.

PLATTNER I think this is the keyword. There is no such world where you can just stick software components together as a kid sticks together Lego building blocks. But there is also no such world in which you can stick software components together as every technically interested teenager does with PC components. The software is much more complicated.

In very simple cases, the PC model could be adequate, but in general, it is not because the software component problem is significantly more complicated. In addition to the aspect that the components beyond the interface must understand the semantic content of the information, there is also the aspect that the systems must meet certain security requirements. I am thinking here not only about the user requirements, but also about the operational relevance of the content that is carried over the interface. There must be a superior authority that ensures this operational security. This demands an enormous expense in engineering.

The illustration of an airplane therefore fits much better than that of an automobile. A car is indeed also a complex technical product, but the focus is essentially on the production. A car is built once and then in essence not ever changed. It will just be repaired. An airplane, in contrast, will be significantly changed in its component parts over its life span of 25 years. On an aircraft, I can install other engines, I can change the electronics, I can alter the interior fittings, and so forth. I therefore like the analogy of aircraft construction much better for software engineering.

You see at once that the aircraft builder has the overall responsibility that the interplay of all the components results in a safe airplane. It is of no importance which components he builds himself, but rather he is concerned that the airplane as a whole is safe. The regulations in this field are very strict because an airplane accident is usually fatal for those involved. There is a real threat here, a worst-case scenario, that must be

Roles in the aircraft industry

avoided under all conditions. Consider the distribution of the system in components and the interworking of the components as background.

There are significant communication flows in an aircraft; that is, the semantic exchange volume in an airplane is quite high, but still several orders of magnitude below what we have in business administration software. What is clear from our illustration is that nobody gets the idea that he can assemble an airplane in his garage because, after all, an airplane is put together from components through definite interfaces. Nobody gets the idea that they can use the Lego image to build an airplane. Actually, we should take the number of interfaces in an airplane and the semantic complexity of these interfaces and evaluate them in comparison with the interfaces within an SAP R/3 system. With airplane construction, nobody has the idea of building one at home in his garage, just because of the safety aspect— that is, because he could not find a test pilot.

Because this is so, an engineering community is formed. Some of them do the design for the overall aircraft, and they have the responsibility for making sure the product can be sold on the market, that is, that there is a market for the product. Others are concerned with aircraft maintenance and set-up service worldwide, and they are responsible for the infrastructure. Others are responsible for the way the individual components work together; they make some of the components themselves and order others from component manufacturers.

The model of the virtual company

A brisk engineering exchange takes place between the airplane manufacturer and the component manufacturers and also between the component manufacturers themselves. They work together to make the interfaces fit. This virtual company brings the component manufacturers together. Both the airplane manufacturer and the component manufacturers contribute to the work of the engineering team. It is totally unthinkable that you would simply choose components from the catalog, shove them together, and have the control system for the engines in this aircraft.

SCHEER Would this not be the model for software development in the future, Mr. Wendt? Where you say, the partners know each other, they agree among themselves, and a partner is only allowed into such an engineering association when he has proven his quality and has also shown solid planning for the future that guarantees he will remain available as a partner over the long haul. In this way, you build development networks that also have a strategic significance, where the partners cannot be exchanged at will.

This illustration with component libraries on the Internet, where you can find components that you just assemble into a system, must be rejected as unrealistic.

WENDT Yes, that is how it is. Mr. Plattner is totally correct. The illustration of the complicated large aircraft is the proper image. There are, however, large organizations that are responsible overall, whether it is Airbus Industries or Boeing, and that deliver the aircraft. They do not, of course, manufacture all the components themselves but instead order tires or wheels for the landing gear, for example. The engineers in the big company necessarily confer with the engineers in the smaller supplier companies because the interface compatibility works only with direct information exchange. The landing gear specialists of the supplier know certain things better than the overall designer at Boeing. Despite this fact, however, in the final analysis the overall responsibility still lies with Boeing.

I see SAP in analogy with Boeing. There are a lot of small component suppliers, but they do not just put their components in a catalog so that you can order them as if it were the Quelle department store. They

SAP in analogy with Boeing

clarify matters with SAP about what interfaces they are supplying components for. Also keep in mind the question about how long a supplier company must be available; it is a little different with hardware than it is with software. If you leave it the way it is now, that in many software source texts only the programmer knows his way around and otherwise nobody else, then you really have to send a prayer up to heaven that the programmer lives as long as possible and that you will still have access to him. This miserable situation should really be brought to an end in the foreseeable future.

We have to reach a point, as is obviously the case in the aircraft industry, where you can reach back to the engineering plans, so when the developer is no longer available, you can return to the documentation and implement the decisions of the developer. I see the situation with large-scale software, the complex software, in exactly the same way that Mr. Plattner sees it.

Engineers versus mathematicians

I feel that many scientists cannot see things in information science this way because they came out of mathematics. In mathematics, there are no urgent tasks to be performed. In mathematics, a person tries his proof, and if it works, it is good, and if it does not work out, he has had bad luck. But he cannot hire 2,000 people and say, now we will prove this with 2,000 people.

With aircraft construction, in contrast, we know that a great many specialists with different special knowledge are involved, and it is the same way with large-scale software. Therefore Mr. Plattner, as an engineer, looks at things in a totally different way from a mathematician. And I believe that this way of looking at things is absolutely necessary.

PLATTNER But the obverse is certainly not correct, that a mathematician could not work as an engineer.

WENDT Of course, a mathematician can become an engineer.

PLATTNER At SAP, there are many examples of this: Henning Kagermann, a theoretical physicist; Klaus Tschira, an experimental physicist; Peter Zencke, a mathematician and business administrator; or Hopp— no, he is an engineer.

SCHEER Moreover, there are also tasks in mathematics that you have to break up and do in parallel in order to accomplish them in any reasonable amount of time. I am thinking here of large-scale optimization systems, not of proving theorems, but of the computer management behind them.

But I would like to return to our illustration once more because we have said that we want to examine this comparison about where the two agree and do not agree. In the aircraft industry, we have found good parallels as far as handling the complexity, but this is in fact a different type of product development or production. There are repetitive processes involved. This is just not the case with software.

Partnerships in the software industry

With software, it is always just research and development partnerships, whereas in the aircraft industry, a component manufacturer brings in its production capabilities along with the development capabilities because he has the machines and the production know-how. This is not the case with software development. A partner, once he has brought in his know-how, cannot fall back repetitively on his production resources, but rather must bring in new know-how in order to be interesting for a partnership again.

PLATTNER Let us take the partnerships that SAP has, the partnerships with the data bank producers or the partnership with the producer of office components.

We have had partnerships with the data bank producers for 15 years now. There are indeed always further developments, sometimes significant developments of both a technical kind and a logical kind. We must always adjust to these. So this is very analogous to the procedures in aircraft development with the replacement of the engines or the replacement of the control electronics or the navigational electronics. That is based to a large degree on what you have put together the last time and is not entirely new. But there is nonetheless so much new in it that a significant engineering expense is required in order to develop a new combination.

So I think that there is such a thing as products that are components in the software being sold and being built—components that you must examine over long years ahead in terms of the next large-scale integration and that you must develop jointly with the suppliers and the users.

SCHEER Let us go back a bit in history. Earlier, we had the following vertical structure with hardware: A hardware manufacturer built everything, from the processor up to the peripherals. Meanwhile, however, there is a horizontal structure in which some producers make the chips, others make the boards, the next one makes yet something else, and finally the big boys assemble the components into the systems. This actually works, because what Mr. Wendt said applies: The less semantics an interface has, the easier it is to break things down into components.

The hardware and software branches

With hardware, we are at the technical level where signals are being exchanged that you can describe relatively simply. With our content applications, where an exchange of strongly semantic specifics is taking place, there still perhaps is a need, alongside the trend to separate a system into components, for the partners to have special knowledge.

PLATTNER Because of this, the communications portion can be more expensive than building the components.

SCHEER Yes, but despite this, there is always an effort to achieve standardization.

PLATTNER This is right. We are seeing that right now with the new dimension applications, that is, the Business Information Warehouse (BW), the Sales Force Automation (SFA), or the Advanced Planner and Optimizer (APO). The communications system between them, as Peter Zencke called it once, is not only the plug connection of the system, but rather the process that synchronizes the systems so that they are able to exchange information. What do they have to know? Let us take an Advanced Planner and Optimizer system and an R/3 system. What do they have to know about each other in order to talk with each other at all?

Semantic synchronization

They must at least know for what companies they are working, in what environment they are working. A whole list of descriptive basic data must be accessible for the APO system from the R/3 system because otherwise, the components do not know in what context they are being employed; that is, the components would not be synchronized. The Advanced Planner and Optimizer then would not understand the information conveyed for the most part in coded format because it could not decode it. For example, it would not know where accounting district 07 is, if it does not know that accounting district 07 happens to be England. Once we called this synchronization semantic synchronization, and it demands a significant outlay in costs.

We humans also must first practice that before we can truly communicate. We are indeed both speaking German, but we must first always adjust our world of concepts so that we know what we mean when we use certain words. When we say "city," for example, it could be that we mean some big city, a small city, or specifically the city of Berlin. When we have agreed that we are talking about Berlin, then it is clear that we mean Berlin when we just say "city."

This same type of synchronization must take place between the systems, and at least the exchange of the information that this synchronization serves must be standardized, or otherwise the systems will talk past each other. In a network of applications components, there are not just two partners, but rather we see just in our network at least ten times as many systems that should more or less freely communicate with each other. So we have to make some significant expenditures for the semantic coordination for all the communicating components to be at the same point where the basic concepts are concerned.

Componentware **SCHEER** So here we have the antithesis where everyone talks to you through componentware and you can see the advantages—but on the other hand, the coordination expenses with these components can, after all, be so great that under some circumstances a centralized solution would be simpler.

PLATTNER Yes, at least where you have the centralized engineering responsibility for the integration of the components. We also see very clearly where the integration of components progresses rapidly, namely where the interface does not have to know much about what is going back and forth. This is the case, for example, with Office Objects. When I connect an Office Object, that is, text, with a business transaction, then our transaction does not know what is in the text; only the reader knows the meaning of the text.

SCHEER The same is true for the data bank. It also has no entry into the semantics of the content.

PLATTNER At the beginning, we had the illustration with the digital camera and the photo from the ship's mast. There the data stream from the technical system was not interpreted at all. The interfaces over which the image was sent are relatively simple. Therefore the integration goes very fast in such systems. By way of contrast, the integration between SAP and a planning system such as I2 or Manugistics requires a significant expenditure, even with the interface of the first generation, where everyone knew that it was still not satisfactory.

The idea is totally unrealistic for me that you can simply stick together business administration components that have a much higher complexity than the simple office applications. You can figure on the expense of the merger being as high as, or even higher than, it is for the production of the components themselves. This is exactly the point where you have to think about whether you will build such components yourself, even when there are already such components.

In the future, I believe, an industry will slowly, but surely, be created that will sell complete components to others without having any relationship to the customers. They will supply a customer who will house other components around the original components and then make a product for the end user.

SCHEER The question is whether this complexity that we have described here is based on the business applications or whether it is a result of not having established any standardization. Nobody can tell me that accounting is something so terribly complicated. It is only that you have free space, a degree of freedom, in the application, and you have to know a lot about how this degree of freedom will be used. There is a lot of discretion in the creation of such an application.

<aside>Again: standards make trouble</aside>

If there were standards, however, about how you would describe the data structures from the standpoint of the content, how you would derive certain algorithms as to how accounting functions, and how cost accounting functions, then I know simply, aha, this cost accounting will subsequently be developed in accordance with the DIN [German Industrial Norms]. I then do not need to know anything further about how it works in detail because it is standardized. And I believe that this is a restrictive factor that is not absolutely necessary. I do not believe that the business applications necessarily have to be so different in all cases; I can imagine standards throughout.

Possibly industry standards will be implemented, and then I simply know, aha, this follows the style of SAP accounting; then I do not need to think any further about it because I know the work method. If this becomes the global standard, I can even connect various components. As long as this is not the case, however, I evidently have a high level of complexity, one that is not absolutely necessary. It has already been said that we are beginning to achieve standards where you already know the contents very well or where they are simple.

PLATTNER Yes, but the spirit of a fundamental change now prevails and even penetrates the most complicated realms. For example, the Product Data Management (PDM) is where design systems, engineering CAD systems, and the manufacturing, administrative, and planning systems, as we build them, come together. Indeed a significant complexity of information is exchanged here. The question is who is actually responsible for the management system.

SCHEER Yes, that is exactly the question. One puts a system in between. The PDM system is really nothing other than a dictionary that sits between the logistics system and the design system because they cannot understand each other directly. Therefore I place a semantic interface between them.

PLATTNER But how does that look specifically? It will take at least two manufacturers in this field to work together and say, "Now we will solve this problem, and we will solve it in a way that the connection is not an emergency solution, but rather that it is a constructive solution. In doing this, we must also be careful to respect each other and not step on each other's toes and make cooperation more difficult."

I do not know how the automobile industry achieved it, but it would be interesting to check out how Bosch and Daimler made it clear that Bosch would not build any autos, even though Bosch was producing 50 percent of the components of a car. Bosch has no intention of building some tin around these components and offering Bosch cars in competition with Daimler.

By way of contrast, let's take a look at the PC industry. The situation is not too far off from Intel being a PC or computer manufacturer. They actually are building computers, even with the cases, where the buyer can just paste on his own name. Otherwise, the entire, complete piece of equipment is built by Intel. That is already a threat to the other consumers of the Intel components.

The problem in the software industry

That is actually the problem with software; at least, I believe it is. Every software producer knows that in principle every other producer can do what he himself does. It developed differently among the production business where they diverged. But with us, it is this way because software is produced the same way everywhere by similar people. The only thing that differentiates between these people is the circumstance that they have different knowledge in their repositories, that is, in their heads. And perhaps they also have a different team tradition.

SCHEER That is just what I meant before. It is always a matter of research and development partnerships. The other components are lacking what the software component producers would have to have for it to be any different, the production technology. There is none for the software because software developers do not need anything other than their ten fingers. And everyone has those and can start at any time. Because of this, the pressure for sharing the work or the advantage of sharing the work is not at all so obvious.

There are countervailing tendencies. I can outsource, but after some time I can also in-source again. I can try to find a partner who has better know-how. But after some time, I might reconsider whether it would be simpler to integrate the tasks again in my business. It might be that Intel also possibly said to itself, "I started off as a chip manufacturer because the market is broken up horizontally, but later, it may be that I will make cabinets as well and then buy myself a few components from others." Then I can also in-source somewhat more functionality. I therefore believe that you cannot really make any trend predictions. You can only observe the factors that will determine this market and that it might possibly break down into components.

PLATTNER I believe that the next recession in our industry will strongly trigger this. At this time, we have almost no kind of recession or there are no actual crises. Not all the software publishers are doing well, but there is a lot of hope that one can make a breakthrough with a new idea. Everything is being developed rather in parallel direct to the customer. Very few software publishers are concentrating on this or defining it as the business objective to build components that will then be used by other software producers. They are clearly the minority.

I believe that with the next recession our branch suffers, a lot more of these software companies will end up in a crisis situation of competition, so they will have to consider, "Do we really need our own sales, or shouldn't it be an engineering-type sales for those who reuse our components?" We should take a look at how it developed in the automobile industry or in other industries. For example, broadcasting is now 60 years old. How did specialization and the division of labor work in there?

SCHEER Isn't your picture of the software industry too optimistic? The great success of SAP naturally puts everything else that is happening in its shadow. When we take away SAP, we actually have lived through the extinction of the software publishers here in Germany in the past five years. Ten years ago the hardware died off, and two weeks ago Nixdorf was finally buried. The rest that is there, the last few things, will also probably be sold to AT&T.

PLATTNER Yes, but at the same time there are a whole lot of software companies springing up out of the ground in America.

SCHEER Yes, but only where the market can't be taken in at a glance, where there still is no structure. For example, in the area of multimedia, where you can still do something with one small idea and then later perhaps be bought out.

PLATTNER But here we have a classic division. We have the data bank producers, the tool producers, and the applications producer, which overlaps with the tools a bit. There are now a number of data bank producers. They have clearly made it their strategy to make their products for reuse through other software companies, and they have been very successful. And there will still be data banks for the next 30 years.

SCHEER But there is also starting to be movement here. There are even data bank producers who are also doing applications software, and there are applications software businesses that the producers of data bank systems are buying up.

PLATTNER Yes, yes, but because of this, there is still a clear division. The important relationships of SAP, for example, to the data bank producers Oracle, IBM, and Microsoft—we have four data bank suppliers that supply SAP and that works really very well. We have a similar situation with Microsoft Office, and I believe that there will be even more components. The first 10 years, I believe, we foundered around because everyone was saying that they had the repository. IBM came in with SAA, which was strongly based on componentware. But they said, "We have the repository." Of course, it was incompatible with all the others who simultaneously came up with the same idea and said, "In the beginning, there is the repository."

Open repositories

SCHEER And how is it now with Microsoft?

PLATTNER Microsoft also says, "We have the repository." But right from the beginning, Microsoft saw that it could not have all the repositories in the world, so its repositories would have to be able to understand each other. You can, after all, use an object that is not stored in your own repository, but rather in another one. You just have to have the anchor point. The themes are thus open repositories and repository interfaces. Here, too, you must make a couple of basic technological decisions.

The outlook for component manufacturers

I am thinking about the unhappy story of COM and CORBA. Now we have incompatible plugs, and it is a very expensive incompatibility. I believe that half of the components that we could have used were excluded, because they could not be used in the Microsoft world and also in the non-Microsoft world, or that we would have had to build two plugs in the world at that time instead of being able to use one universal plug. If this problem, which to a large degree rests in the hands of IBM and Microsoft, would be resolved, then many of the small software publishers would move more in the direction of also developing components. Not only for the office area, but also for other areas. We are moving in this direction.

Then there are those who overlap each other, and this overlapping has something to do with selection and the market. Those who do not overlap, or who only overlap a little, perhaps have it easier to find a partner and thus can increase in value. It is a bit as if the decathlon athlete who does as many things as possible is relatively better off than the specialist. But if the market situation changes, if the way of thinking about components in the area of larger components takes hold and becomes a significant influence, then I believe that component producers could achieve a similar importance as, for example, Bosch or General Electric, who themselves build no cars or airplanes.

Chapter 4

To Travel New Paths: Software Engineering and Management

In many books you can read that the employee is the most important thing, and so on, but you also have to do something about it. And SAP has, I believe, done better than some other businesses. We do not let ourselves be steered by some management cookbook. SAP is not perfect, but it is still a great business.

Walldorf, October 23, 1998

PLATTNER I would like to say something about the newest development of SAP, about the R/3 New Dimension development and business scenarios. For the first time, I have coined a phrase, the term *business scenarios*. Exactly how do we do a total examination from the viewpoint of a user when the software is housed in many different separate systems? This idea is influenced by the Internet. It has established itself with us, and we have made a breakthrough in our thinking.

Defining the problem

We formed the concept of business scenarios on a flight to Los Angeles and changed our presentation charts right on the airplane. When we board, members fly together; we are extremely productive. When we publicly presented the results of our considerations, there was a little confusion on the market at first because our pricing is also connected with this, but then people began to grasp what we had invented.

SCHEER This fits in well with our discussion of software architecture.

PLATTNER Yes, that is a software architecture story. In accordance with our idea, SAP now builds components and applications. We saw that the New Dimension applications have very specific relationships to each other.

SCHEER This can also be a chance for a software publisher to find a way out of the problem of limited capacity because you often think faster than you can develop. If I now say, however, that I have business scenarios and I describe solutions, then the solutions do not always have to consist of 90 or 95 percent of software I have produced myself. I can work much more rapidly with component manufacturers and thus offer solutions faster than I could have earlier with purely my own development.

PLATTNER That is true only as a tendency.

SCHEER It does require that you have standards in the descriptions of such solutions and later also standards for developing and coupling components.

PLATTNER We talked about this subject in our previous conversations. Standards come very late, very slowly, and will be changed 10 times before they stabilize somehow.

A new product family: New Dimension

I would like to explain briefly what we have done at SAP. We have a development in R/3 that is essentially marked by two requirements. On one hand, these requirements come from the IBUs, the branch solutions, which elicit changes in our core applications. On the other hand, there are requirements for improving usability. These are the two current changes in our developments at this time.

Moreover, for a year and a half or two years now, we have started to build satellite systems around the R/3 system. The satellite systems were independent of each other. They indeed used architectures that make it possible for them to communicate, but they were not just parts of one product; each was considered a single product. SAP became a multi-product company. We resumed these satellite developments again in the summer of this year. We designated all of them as products of one family with the name New Dimension. This is really just a "branding," but the fact that we did this makes it obvious that they have a lot in common. They even have a lot more to do with each other than we previously thought.

It is just not true that the individual special applications being made today by niche manufacturers, and also by the best-of-breed manufacturers, do not have anything to do with the other components of a system. They only appear to have nothing to do with each other because they cannot communicate with each other. We saw that we would need solutions such as the BW (Business Information Warehouse) in practically all the applications. This led to the point where we said, "We will not force the developers to bring all these applications back together again on a core system like R/3 because it would drag out the development over time." We would much rather make this split and, on one hand, develop things rapidly and, on the other hand, harmonize things afterwards as much as possible, even at the cost of duplicate development.

The development strategy

For these new applications, we must first of all define the objects being exchanged that must coordinate with each other and with the R/3. We thus have to devote ourselves more to designing and harmonizing these exchange objects. For example, we use the object "customer" in the Business Information Warehouse, and we need it in APO (Advanced Planner and Optimizer), we need it in SFA (Sales Force Automation System), we need it in service, and we need it in marketing. So it is needed everywhere. Can it always be a different object, or is it just a variant of one and the same object? Naturally, it is a matter of variants, various viewpoints of one and the same customer. Now there is a technical harmony established for it. That is the usual data processing development. First various parts are developed separately, and then you pull them back together. This is how the process has run throughout the history of applications development.

Still, something new arrived. We said that we would let these applications exist as standalone applications, even when we harmonize them. They have their own data bank and their own repository available to them. Nevertheless, they must also be a communication system in connection with the other components. We must therefore define the exchange objects in the various repositories. In this way, the systems will remain self-sufficient, but they can also include various software technologies, such as ILOG for mathematical optimization in APO, the ESRI for GIS systems in BW, or Excel for matrix reporting and SFA for palmtop communications.

From a system viewpoint to that of the user

Until now, we have always developed the applications for their specific user group. But then we faced the question about who actually owned the Business Warehouse. Is it a system? Aha, it is a standalone system. But if I am an APO user and want to do optimization, don't I need the market data? I need information about the existing installed base at the time, the immediate sales potential, and the market potential overall. So I need an entry into the Business Warehouse.

We said to ourselves that we have to duplicate the Business Warehouse and integrate it into the Advanced Planner and Optimizer as a component. This leads to the situation where the same component, Business Warehouse, exists both as a standalone product and as a component of the Advanced Planner and Optimizer. Then we saw the Business Warehouse also was needed in the SAP Focus initiative. It concerns what happens around the customer, that is, marketing, sales, and service.

Then the developers in the field of computer science began to build management cockpits. They were based on the Business Warehouse. Naturally, you ask just where the Business Warehouse is located. The answer is typical for the structure in the R/3 system: There is physically only one Business Warehouse and all the applications that use it are "guests" in this Business Warehouse. They assemble their functions there. They have their own data inventories, their reports, their menus, and so on, but they stay in this one system. We actually supply a number of components and then use them many times. We have given this multiple-use concept the name business scenarios.

Multiple uses of a component

Let us take the sales force as an example of a user group. They should essentially work with the data inventory of the sales force automation system. That data inventory is replicated from all the other systems and can go on the laptop through a replication mechanism. And you can work well with it there.

But now the sales employee also wants to access the marketing data in the Business Warehouse. He has two options: He can produce an Excel spreadsheet workbook and let it be delivered over the distribution mechanism. Then he has the data on the laptop. He can also open a window and work directly on the Business Warehouse with the menus in the applications room that we have developed for him.

This business scenario is basically a menu whose contents reflect that of the New Dimension applications and that of the R/3 that are of interest to this employee in sales. This is different from before when we would build an encyclopedic menu. Unfortunately, we did this for too long in R/3 because we always thought that the users would make their own menus. But they do not make them. Therefore, we are now building a Business Scenario menu. It is a complete menu that contains everything in the appropriate context. It is not

The business scenario menu

restricted to a physical data processing system that is identified by exactly one IP number. You might be interested in a transaction in R/3, such as tracking a task through the production and the assembly. The information on the status belonging to this transaction depends on the industry. The salesman might have to call up the Advanced Planner and Optimizer system to make an Availability-to-Promise check so he can say, for example, whether the 200 PCs ordered by a customer can be delivered in two weeks.

The role concept

The user is described by roles. This is the same principle used in our worldwide training, the role-based end-user training. We describe the user or the user group, and we describe the appropriate menu. A flexibility lets each user put together his own submenu within a few minutes. He can change this submenu every day. The salesman basically works with his main system, sales force automation, but he can also access the other components without even knowing that he is leaving the system.

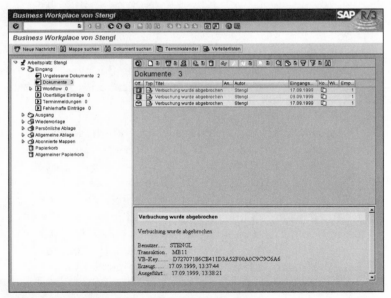

Personalized R/3 workplace (Release 4.6).

To do this, we must ensure that all these applications get a unified corporate design that strongly diverges from today's more technical Windows 95 design. We are coming up with our own design. Wherever you go in these New Dimension applications or in R/3, the design looks the same. The transactions are built differently. The New Dimension applications are built more for the operative user and not for the specialized user in the back office. One goal with many of these applications is to ensure intuitive use without learning expense. They therefore look totally different. The navigation looks different, but the corporate design will look the same.

The business scenario is thus a virtual coupling together of applications. And it naturally comes from what the Internet has already done. There, groups of pointers and URLs are managed, and in the presentation you have the impression that a universal application is behind this, even though the data and the actual applications parts might be distributed everywhere. When they are at least available in one menu system— that is, when I can get to them with a single call-up and when they are halfway similar in design—then I do not experience any leaps in design, and it remains an applications system for me. Even when I do have leaps in design, I can live with that because we will endure it in any case in the future world of electronic commerce, where we work in other, unfamiliar systems.

The Internet as model

SCHEER Can I bring up the relationship to software architecture once again? Could you even say a little maliciously that the componentware idea has been set back somewhat because the integrating movement, centralization, is still too strong?

Contemplate the component idea anew

PLATTNER Yes. I believe that the componentware story about which we spoke earlier does not work in any case, at least from the user's standpoint. It functions at the level of the software producer and at the level of the developer who wants to use components. For example, in GUI development, class libraries were exchanged, but to have all the applications simply agree with each other? To do this, the objects exchanged, which fly back and forth between these applications, must be known to everyone and standardized. We are on the way to accomplishing this. We are doing something in this direction, but we certainly are always lagging behind the applications. Standardization will only help us to reduce costs subsequently.

For three years now, we have been creating a user layer around SAP that uses BAPIs. This is likewise true for New Dimensions, which also has BAPIs. But the important thing is, as Peter Zencke once clearly described in a presentation, we need a semantic integration that goes far beyond the technical connection possibilities. The integration is simple for the abstract objects text, fax, letter, spreadsheet, or image.

WENDT Because there is hardly any semantics in them.

PLATTNER Yes, little.

WENDT You basically only have to talk about the syntax.

PLATTNER Yes.

SCHEER We could sum it up that componentware is not for the user, but is at most something for the software developer and the assembler.

PLATTNER Naturally, it is good for the automobile manufacturer that an exhaust system manufacturer will produce all the variants for him. For the end customer, this matter is no interest at all, whether VW makes the exhaust system itself or it is produced by, for example, Eberspächer.

The SAP component strategy

SCHEER In relation to R/3, this means that the standalone nature of the components within the system makes sense only when other "assemblers" can put these components together in an overall solution. Who could take on this task?

*

PLATTNER There could be partners who take over these tasks. We already are building our applications components Business Information Warehouse, Advanced Planner and Optimizer, and InfoDB in parallel and then harmonizing them. We are not implementing all of them on the same platform. That is the conservative approach of R/3. But it is too slow in a world where everything is rapidly changing and the next thing sometimes follows hot on the heels of the first, where there are new types of communications between businesses and where knowledge is more tightly bound into it.

I therefore believe that the New Dimension approach is tailor-made for when we have to develop these components rapidly and then harmonize them with the back end. We take these additional expenses for harmonization as the cost for being fast. These components therefore have a standalone nature.

SCHEER You save much with the R/3 system when it has more standalone components that also are independent. They can be integrated with other components and they can access common data definitions. They can also have their own data stored and maintained in their own data bank so that they are independent of any changes in the common part in later releases.

PLATTNER We have gained an enormous degree of freedom here, inasmuch as we can also use all the other programming languages simultaneously, Visual Basic, C++, and Java, as well. This makes it easier to incorporate the components that others have built, such as the ILOG components, where components in the software have great importance among the software publishers. ILOG presents itself as a component builder. ILOG builds finished applications only to win projects but basically sees itself as a company that builds components to supply to others.

This will amount to about the same thing as the relationship between Bosch and the automobile manufacturers.

There is a "yes" vote for the idea of components, but not where I can call up various companies, buy a few components, and have a business scenario. I would not have one. I believe that an integrated design must describe a look and feel right through the navigation that actually takes place in a business scenario. The technical integration must be built afterwards.

SCHEER What will the businesses that provide such solutions look like? Will this mean a metamorphosis of present-day software publishers, or could it also mean that new businesses come in from outside, ones that have strong control over the appropriate content knowledge, so that business scenarios are developed starting with the content and then assembling components?

Electronic catalogs **PLATTNER** Content business, that is very stylish now. It ends up in catalogs and I can operate with the catalogs. The catalog is an interface the user can work with. Behind the catalog where he identifies something are data he can use as parameters to compose a transaction and put things together automatically. You can see that now in the B2B scenario.

Only when we have understood that we cannot build a business-to-business solution alone, but rather that we must include a lot of other people, will we make progress. Including them does not mean finding one partner, but rather finding a great number of partners. A partner is, for example, the producer of the broker software Commerce One. He thought that he could do everything, but he covers only a small part with his solution. You have to make a direct connection with some partners. For example, we are directly connected with Amazon.com. When we execute an Amazon.com transaction, the SAP transaction automatically begins.

When you work with the Grainger catalog and order spare parts, an SAP system stands behind this Grainger catalog, but this is not a prerequisite. We thought that it would be a prerequisite, but it is not. We work completely on the basis of the Grainger catalog and find so much information in this catalog that we must deal with the producer of the catalog to take the information and almost automatically support our transaction. The idea that you do a business transaction only once can finally be a reality. And the catalogs play a very important role in this. Some businesses will build catalogs and market them. Others will buy catalog software and develop a catalog in which they put the content, such as Grainger. Aspect sells ready-made catalog inventories, for example, for electronics parts. You can build this outfitted catalog right into your IT system. Companies will put out their own internal catalogs; for this you need catalog software where you can feed in the internal framework requirements, for example, for PCs, software, or the purchase of office supplies.

SCHEER This was always kind of the accusation that people made of the ERP systems, especially in America, that you had to put out a lot of money for something that only made work for you. You bought a system that made it possible to manage the basic data about customers, but first you had to dump in all the customer data or enter the entire inventory of items. In contrast, if I buy a catalog along with the system, then I can immediately support my business processes.

PLATTNER I believe that for a long time you have been able to buy objects such as "customer" or "special customer in an industry." We load them into the system through interfaces. I believe that we will work this way in the future as well. You have the data in a catalog and click it and then receive as much data as you want. You do not have to capture it or enter it. The catalog business is flourishing. Once we also wanted to do something like this, but we did not find the impetus for it. Meanwhile, it really does not matter who does it. There are many companies showing up whose business idea is to do a catalog for certain fields.

For example, the retail branch has a lot of various people and various paths. The very small shop, the specialty shop, has to figure out for itself how to deal with things, and its quality resides in the fact that it has put together an interesting inventory. Then there is mail-order business through catalogs, there are department stores, the warehouse, there are special businesses, the boutiques—there are many possible ways in which you can sell things. Now everything is coming out in electronic form on the Internet. It is quite clear here that the integration of others' components is mandatory here. It does not matter whether they are physically integrated into the offer or whether they are fully independent of each other. The integration of these components is a very essential aspect of future software.

SCHEER And what effect on things do matters of quality, time, costs, and security have?

PLATTNER That is a good question. The coupling with another's system takes place over a rather narrow interface, and because it is so narrow and relatively simple, it is also secure.

SCHEER That depends, however, on whether you have a concentration on such primitive interfaces for the application.

PLATTNER Yes, and when the interface is broader, then we get the EDI problem. It will become more difficult, it will cost more, and it will therefore lead to pushing for standardization more rapidly because many people are participating and want to save on costs.

SCHEER The pressure for standardization will simply be greater.

PLATTNER Standardization is not the enabler with which something can be done, but rather standardization only comes in later. Cell phones grew without standardization, and now they all have the problem that the European cell phone does not function in America and the American one does not work here. Therefore, they released the super-cell phone that works in both regions. The world is like that and it is probably a good thing, because otherwise we would constantly be working with norms and stay stuck in the past.

Back to the question of the product. When we put together a business scenario and sell this business scenario; then it is also understood that we are responsible for its quality. We are responsible, independently of the question of whether we made certain parts of the software ourselves or whether we purchased them. We are responsible for the whole, even if it is really just a virtual whole. I can't grab hold of it, but it is still a thing. I can perhaps burn it onto a CD-ROM because I can deliver several applications on it. Our philosophy up until now has been that we put everything into just one application and thus guarantee its quality, but our philosophy is undergoing a change in that we are putting several applications into a package and still must guarantee the quality of the whole.

SCHEER I can remember very well, and it is not too far in the past, when SAP always avoided getting into being the general contractor. But now we are automatically getting into such a situation.

PLATTNER Yes, and we are also seeing a new class of problems. This does not happen without some costs involved. These components, even if we have built them ourselves, can't just be stuck together. There are naturally component integration problems and standards problems because, for example, two development groups have different ideas about who the customer is and how the system should be presented to him. If this agreement does not meet 100 percent, it leads later to annoyance for the user.

Components
and complexity

SAP works in international teams.

SCHEER What effect will this then have on the speed of development? Don't we have to employ simultaneous engineering and concurrent engineering with the suppliers to coordinate the release cycles with each other?

PLATTNER It is for just this reason that we start with few components. We will soon have to establish this rhythm with all of them. The same problem exists as well between the basic development and the applications development. Something that has always been a problem in the past has been the transverse section projects in which a change affects several components and they must be modified to the new condition one after the other. The problem of synchronization comes to the forefront here. This problem area has been increased multifold through including partners.

One thing is better than before. There are more employees working overall in the world. There are far more workers in the field of software development. We can achieve a higher starting quality, and the coupling of the system is much better. We can get to the next higher level of complexity. Because one thing is very clear: It will become even more complex. I always say this. Anyone who believes that components will make anything simpler does not understand anything about software development.

WENDT That is also the tendency in other technical fields. When you want to make it simpler for the customer, for the actual user, so the complexity of the implementation increases for the engineer. With an old car, you had to double-clutch to shift gears, and the transmission design was very simple for the engineer. Today, in contrast, you drive with an automatic transmission and you do not perform the coupling any more. The driver has it much simpler, and he does not even have to know how to shift gears any more. But for the engineer, it has become many times more complicated to build an automatic transmission, and it will always go on that way. It always has to be an advantage for the customer that it becomes simpler and acquires an interesting functionality. The engineer who has to implement the improvement must master an ever-growing complexity.

The user's joy, the developer's sorrow

PLATTNER For many years, we built R/3 for the professional user and now we are serving the occasional user. We have to be much more oriented toward these new classes of users. In the final analysis, all employees will work, will have to work, with the system more or less. This creates real pressure for the New Dimension applications. In creating a business scenario, we must imagine, for example, a field service employee and ask ourselves what he expects to happen when he pushes a certain button. We have to make things easier for the user wherever we can. As a consequence, there must be more programming in the background. The best solution is not the cheapest, but rather the one with the fewest user adaptation costs for whatever user class is being considered at the time. And this places a massive amount of pressure on R/3 development when it is subjected to these criteria from the user side.

What counts today is not the technology, but being useful to the user

SCHEER It was quite revealing to me that at the beginning, you described a software architecture without using a single technical concept, just by speaking of business scenarios. The technology in software development, or in information science in general, is probably less and less important as an argument in and of itself. The technical concept of client/server was perhaps the last technical argument that you could still use to promise a benefit for the user.

PLATTNER The Internet as a technology has had this effect. But now the Internet is becoming simply the work platform that you cannot do without.

SCHEER Component architecture or object orientation will not, in any case, be the draft horse that you can use as a justification to pull the user into a leap of generations in the software.

PLATTNER This is, however, the same with the other big leaps in technology, such as the introduction of carbon into aircraft construction, automobile construction, or ship construction. "I will only take a ship that is a carbon ship," is an argument that doesn't work. But carbon is used where it is appropriate and where its properties have the desired effect. Anyone who does not use object-oriented technology where it can productively be used faces a disadvantage in production. This can be a crucial disadvantage, even when it amounts to only about 3 percent.

SCHEER There are, however, ERP providers who still use such arguments.

PLATTNER Naturally, even Audi, when it introduced the new Audi A8, put the "space-frame technology" where you can weld aluminum, right out in front. But it loses its importance because in the meantime, others can also weld aluminum, and others also are saying that they can make a car just as light with other technology, for example, with carbon. It is totally wrong to fight over the question of whether the carbon auto or the aluminum space-frame auto is better. The battle must be fought on the question of what car drives better, looks better, can be serviced more easily, or uses less fuel. The fuel consumption is really the important thing in this connection, and it is what creates the demand that the car be lighter in weight.

SCHEER Yes, but along what lines are the software publishers, the ERP software publishers, now converging? Earlier it was certainly engineering-driven. Then there was the newspaper interview with you, I can see it now, where it said on the front page, "SAP is changing into a marketing-driven business."

PLATTNER Well, I won't let that pass; "marketing-driven" does not apply to us!

SCHEER That is how you were quoted. This is the explanation that you gave Paul Wahl at the time.

PLATTNER But what I meant was very clearly a certain shift in the viewpoint. The ERP software is supported by the IT organization of a business and is required by the CFO. It is used to enable the various elements of a business to operate with each other. So it is built strongly from the viewpoint of the business as a focus. Now we must look harder at the user in our orientation. We were always talking about the end user and then Alan Cooper, who consulted with us on our new design, opened our eyes and said, "Don't always talk about the end user. Say who you mean: Is it Jim, Joe, or Jan? And do you have a specific idea of what training they have, just what job they are performing, what they do every day? When someone, for example, in marketing is constantly engaged in creating advertising texts, what do you think their relationship to your SAP transactions is?"

From a business point of view to a user point of view

For a long time, we thought that if we did the right thing for the business, then the business would make sure that Jane likes SAP, but this is not the case. Perhaps Jane does not like SAP because she says, "I don't like it, I have to know too much, someone else should do it, I will continue to concentrate on writing advertising copy. I am a good copy writer."

The experts like SAP because the functionality is so good, and they can use it to perform certain tasks that are presented from the viewpoint of the business. The occasional users, however, do not like it so much because the system did not ask them anything about what they would like to have. We actually have tasked the business with recruiting these users and training them as long as it takes for them to be able to use the functionality. But now we have a different focus. We must also be concerned with this user.

SCHEER From the engineering, from the inner life of a software publisher, to the outside, right up to the end user. This can take place through classifying the businesses, IBUs, the industries, or through a differentiation of the roles that each individual user takes in the business. He does not necessarily have to take a two-week course in Walldorf to learn a certain operation. He should perhaps only get half an hour's training over the Internet, just in time.

Discovering the end user as the customer

PLATTNER The role-based training is headed right in this direction. This development started when the business software that still ran on the mainframe could also run on the PC. The PC now contains all of the technical components that earlier only the large mainframe software had. This has long since grown together or is understood to have grown together. Now we really have to discover the end user as the customer, and I believe that this is one of the mega-trends for ERP publishers. We have to ask ourselves how we can address the end user through marketing. How do we bring him as a person to SAP, how do we develop our image, how

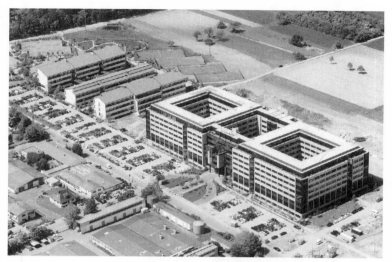

The training center (left) next to the development and sales center (DSC) [EVZ in German] in Walldorf (mid-1990s).

do we present it to him? Our Enjoy activities make a contribution here. For the first time, we are writing to the end users so that they can respond and we get to know them. We have about 3.5 million end users now.

SCHEER Until now, the ERP producer looked at its product as essentially a system and then left the customers to others, namely the implementers and consultant firms who take care of the end customers. If you want to get closer to the customers, a shift is probably necessary in this field and also in understanding the roles between those executing the project and the product manufacturer.

PLATTNER Yes, I see it in exactly the same way. And the exciting thing is that you will, on one hand, have to do all the complicated development about which we have spoken, and on the other hand, everything will be a bit simpler to do.

SCHEER Yes, now it is a matter of the product and the fight for the customers begins.

PLATTNER This fight will take place on a very similar level as with the other consumer goods. The product must have appeal.

Relationship between ERP providers and consulting firms

SCHEER The power relationships are also changing. The consulting enterprises that came out of the accounting companies and have cared for their customers for decades naturally got into this consulting. They have taken advantage of the product. Now you see people who until now have focused on the product and have determined that they must offer their product in variations to be more visible to the consumers. These two groups are running into each other with their strategies. In my opinion, this market will no longer be as clearly divided as before, and you will have people poaching on the other's preserve.

PLATTNER I would not say that they would be poaching. The consulting must be delivered along with the system. As a component that is separately invoiced, to be sure, but it is undisputed that it belongs to the solution. We have just found a structure through Team-SAP in which we are trying to direct our participation, and the participation of the others, in a balanced manner and optimize them for the customer. For the customer, this means that prices go down and quality goes up. A prerequisite for this is that the know-how of the consulting employee, either in-house or outside, should be as high as possible. I believe that we are now closer than ever to each other. We have never been without consulting, but now we are closer to each other and we possibly overlap each other. This does not mean that it can only be A or B, but rather that it is both A and B.

SCHEER We have seen the big consulting firms that earlier also developed software themselves drop the software like a hot potato, for example, Andersen. IBM has dropped out of the applications software market.

PLATTNER They want to hustle back into it.

SCHEER How will this play out? ERP providers are approaching the customer more strongly, developing more solutions, connecting their software with other producers, as well, and they are progressing further with their competence in solutions than in their competence with the product. Could it also be possible that consulting enterprises or hardware-oriented businesses like, for example, IBM are following a similar strategy and becoming assemblers of software components?

The trend toward a solution provider

PLATTNER Yes, naturally. In the final analysis, the one who has the advantage is the one who can assemble things rapidly. I still believe that our main task is to rapidly achieve the solution that we want to achieve with the customer. This is one of the urgent design tasks we have. It has to be to our advantage that we can achieve a functional solution with a guaranteed quality.

Recently, a large enterprise at the last minute broke off a project that had been going on for a number of years and put in an SAP project to make sure that it was Year 2000 compliant. The problem was that the quality was not good enough to achieve that and to meet certain requirements the authorities had set down. I believe that the quality of the solution is a very important criterion. And when you look at the quality of automobiles—I always return to the automobile—it has risen. The absolute quality of autos has risen because in development an engineering department always keeps together everything that deals with quality. The quality checks in purchasing, long testing periods with the prototypes, and with the pre-production cars. Then there are tests during production and tests once again after production. The auto is produced in a large series almost free of error. We see ourselves, now as before, as serial producers with a high level of variability.

SCHEER What do the developers look like who have more of this customer-oriented thinking and who can produce variations from this customer orientation as well?

Customer orientation demands a new type of developer

Are they other types? Do we need a different type of developer than previously?

PLATTNER There will be a change here, just as in the other industries. Another example of customer orientation is a pilot's instrument panel. It was developed with the idea that the pilot had to learn to deal with so many instruments. This was a quality aspect of the pilot, that he could master this complexity. Now you have an about-face; there must be so many pilots in the world because so many aircraft are flying. For this reason, you build only the electronic instruments, the EFIS equipment. Here multiple presentations that are very flexible come from a computer with a screen. On it you can display the weather, the navigation, or the monitoring of an engine. The pilots were heavily involved in planning this. First, one analyzed how a pilot works, what he wants to have, what he can understand, and how much information per second he can absorb, and then the equipment was developed and built.

The new computer center at the development and sales center (DSC) (1992).

SCHEER Yes, but the customer, that is, the pilot, has also changed. Earlier he was a hero who dared to go up in the air and who was the master of a complicated airplane. Today, he is someone who comes out when you leave the airplane and thanks you for flying with him. That is, he also has contact with the customer. Someone once said to me that he would fly for the first time when you give the captain a $2 tip afterwards, because then you would be sure he would have total control of his aircraft, and the pilot would fully lose his aura as an adventurer.

PLATTNER But then they would not call him captain any more. Back to the original question: How do we bridge the gap between the various users of the system and their roles on the one side and our developers on the other side? The original simple idea that we told our developers years ago was for them to get out and go to the end users, but that did not work because the developers do not know what to discuss with them. When a developer builds a component in a component architecture—we have always had a component architecture in our system—then the users are other programs. They are not the end users, but they are other programs that use the component programmed by the developer. He thus has a totally different idea of whom he is actually speaking to.

Bridges between developers and users

We therefore need other people who perhaps are also in development. We have already talked about industry-specific development. For example, in the fields of air travel and defense, we have people who are specialists, who have studied aircraft construction and talk with the aircraft builders. We build software for aircraft builders, that is, for engineers who build aircraft with our software. We need people who actually come out of this culture.

It was always this way in developing the classic applications in back office and in accounting. At the beginning, we started off the same way, and that is how we
got such a good lead out front. We sat down at the
companies, and every day we had this end user contact. Because of our growth, we have somewhat lost
this. Now it is no longer enough to go to the cafeteria
in the businesses involved and talk once with the end
users. Now we have to organize this contact properly,
and we have to build it up and maintain it. And we also
need other talents.

For example, a design enterprise that develops screen
layouts visited here recently. Within a few weeks, they
discovered a whole list of things that we could clearly
do better without having to change our software. But a
lot of detailed work is tied up with this. I can return to
our continuing example of the automobile. Once, many
years ago, Porsche starting using a super design for a
dashboard. It has held up almost to today. At the same
time, there were dashboards that, if you looked at
them today, you would think, "It is impossible what
they expected of the driver." Today all dashboards in
all cars are designed by a team of designers and
ergonomic specialists—and they also try to create a
market individuality so that you can see you are sitting
in a Ford or in a Mercedes. The dashboard has
assumed the importance of the engine parts.

The great Jaguars of the 50s were still designed by Sir
John Lions himself. He was the CEO of Jaguar. In the
beginning, we also did the screen design for our software ourselves. Now we need designer teams. I believe
that the software industry will develop as did other
industries in which such services are performed outside.
There will be cooperation with various experts; that is,
we will give up some things and let others do them or
assign them to other, newly created departments.

We stuck with this original idea for a long time; the
developers at SAP had everything within their grasp,

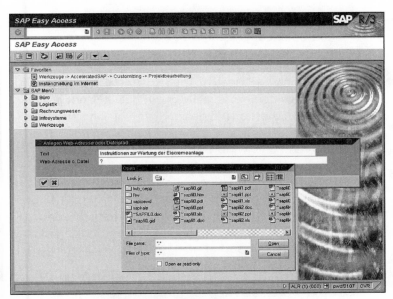

New user interface for R/3 Enjoy (Release 4.6).

from the requirements of the end user right through the performance requirement of the data bank. This was a great advantage that we kept this up for a long time and did not specialize too much at SAP. A great advantage in comparison with the others who thought that one could design the software from a business administration viewpoint and that the other could convert this to the applications code. I believe that this model has never resulted in great products. We were always better positioned, but I believe that now we need specialists along this entire track, for example, for the user interaction design. Today this is a research discipline with knowledge of how people interact and how they deal with complex machines. We also have to use this knowledge in our software products.

SCHEER This field is becoming terribly exciting. The information science concept is expanding when we connect it with the entire responsibility for such a system.

Expansion of the information science concept

PLATTNER Now we are hitting on the subject of why we need other colleges.

SCHEER We have a good transition over to the theme of education and research. The expansion of tasks in software development is really enormous. It is not just a matter of questions of design. I am thinking also, for example, of role-based training that is provided over the Internet. How do you construct such learning units, and what stagecraft do you put into it? We are producing such learning units in Saarbrücken and even hiring theater professionals for them. They tell us how you make stories interesting enough that someone will spend 10 minutes of his lunch break looking at a learning unit instead of going outside and smoking a cigarette.

PLATTNER It must also appear interesting to the somewhat introverted type among the software developers that we are becoming somewhat more multicultural in the software scene. It is no longer enough to say that everyone can do software if he is intelligent enough and has studied information science, mathematics, physics, or something similar, but rather we really need these other qualities as well. This is not making excuses, but is a real necessity. You have to recognize that you are wrong if you think that anyone gets the ability to design along with his mother's milk. You must simply recognize there is a whole playing level above that.

I am also thinking of the specialist we need to be able to install systems rapidly. It is not just a matter of packing up the system and shipping it, but we have to look at the unpacking and ask how that happens. What all has to be done before the software will run? The fact that we have reduced the installation time to a few hours despite the large size of the system is due to the performance of specific people who have a totally different focus. For them, it is not important how the system is programmed and what procedures are contained with it. For them, it is important that the installation procedures work. We are creating new professional specialties. Just think about the variations on designer. There is an enormous spectrum from Dreamworks to Excel.

SCHEER Perhaps Mr. Wendt can report on how he evaluates the current status of education in information science, in comparison with the US as well, and where he sees shortcomings. And perhaps you will also tell us how you came up with the idea of founding a course of studies in software engineering and what is behind it.

Shortcomings in the information science education

WENDT The complaints about the shortcomings in information science education come from companies that deal with very complex software. In information science, you have difficulties in coping with such large-scale systems from the scientific standpoint when you come out of college, which is also what they told me in America. The enterprises that develop such systems shut themselves off in their buildings and do not let the students in. We are talking here about real products the size of R/3 or a bit smaller, in any case of more than one million lines of source code. In college, you basically work only with much smaller units. What was not so clear to me before, but what has now been said to me by many sources in the US, is the judgment that the concept of software engineering is viewed in a negative way in scientific circles.

SCHEER Because it is difficult to subject it to scientific examination.

WENDT Yes, as long as you are dealing with mathematics, the quality of scientific work is generally easy to judge. It is particularly easy if the assessment is based on numbers. When you do a series of experiments and then evaluate the statistics, and you can say that one is 30 percent better than the other, the quality of the solution is immediately recognized. About 90 or 95 percent of the academic activities you read in the publications are determined in this way. When Americans

Strained relations between information science and software engineering say that almost all the treatises in the field of software engineering to date are poor when measured by the usual scientific standards, then it certainly has something to do with the concepts of practicality or testing that are hard to grasp in the practice of science.

The critics might be right that in the field of software engineering, there has been hardly anything you really have to take seriously. The relationship between mathematics-oriented information scientists and software engineers reminds me a bit of the relationship between trained doctors and healing practitioners who insist that certain things cannot be healed through classic medicine. You have to address the illness in a totally different way. The mathematics-oriented information scientists look down on the software engineers because supposedly they lack a solid scientific background. The software engineers in return accuse the mathematics-oriented information scientists of busying themselves with interesting questions at their high scientific level, but ones that have little importance for the practical work. That is the situation today, which is fortunately being admitted by more and more information scientists working in mathematics.

SCHEER Information scientists working in mathematics have not taken into account such complex ERP systems. I have also noted this in my discipline, concerned with applications, as well. There you discuss procedure models and similar things in software engineering without ever having seen real standard software. Until recently, it was also said that the sole option for implementing an information system in an enterprise was to develop it yourself. Modifying a standard system through customizing was not recognized as a problem at all, and nobody at the university knew anything about it.

WENDT In information science, the idea prevails that you must develop an entire system from the ground up, starting with some requirements. This will work from the content standpoint with three or four people. I have often declared that information science education is only good when three or four people later operate their own software company. It is, however, not education for engineers who can work in a company where thousands of software engineers make their contribution to one large-scale system, as is the case with SAP. That requires a very different education.

SCHEER You had to integrate information scientists trained in that way here at SAP, and you did, in fact, succeed in that or else SAP would not have been so successful. But then something must have happened here to convince you to say that you can improve on things somewhat and that this has happened through new research and educational ways.

PLATTNER We have said more than once that we will take a look at what engineering education looks like. Engineering education begins with mathematics and physics in a harmonic, closed, almost abstract world. By contrast, the world of the engineer is always more complicated. You only stay in this closed world when you go into transistor technology and remain in physics after all. If you, in contrast, go into the construction of electronics equipment, for example, then suddenly you face other problems. I am thinking here about a guy in Karlsruhe who once built an oscillator for 10MHz. There had to be a front panel on it with tuning knobs—which had nothing to do with the oscillator. That means that the piece of equipment to be provided is a solution and that it goes far beyond the inner core.

The information scientist lives in an ideal world

The problem in information science and with software developers is that they grew up in a mathematical abstract world in which you can solve almost everything. This world is, however, a long ways away from the real solutions.

PLATTNER You could have them, though, because the systems were in fact there. One goes ever further into the limited mathematical model world. Let's take object orientation. That is a purist model to represent the reality. What I want to say here is that the reality can never be represented that way. This will not be reality. In reality, you need a designer. A designer is not included in object orientation. We already hear very critical voices. For example, the repair friendliness of a piece of software equipment is not determined by its object-oriented programming, but you have to think in terms of exchangeable components.

SCHEER The object orientation has in the meantime been overtaken by the composition paradigms.

PLATTNER I believe that you can recognize very clearly from what we have just described that a software system is something more complicated than the sum of a well-programmed algorithm. Therefore I see the necessity that we not approach it from a mathematical-scientific, almost abstract angle. We need the mathematical abstract world in the way that the electronic engineer needs physics and mathematical education. He is only trained as an engineer, however, when he can build systems. This includes at least knowing what requirements will be placed on design in the future. Even if you work afterwards at another job, you have to know that the component-user interaction is relatively great. We are not allowed to adjust it somehow as much as we possibly can. This component will play a great role in our systems because the systems communicate worldwide and millions of people must deal with this. Our pressure comes from this. There are also software developers who develop the applications interactions. These requirements also fit into our image of this profession.

Let us look at Dreamworks. It is tremendous what all can today be simulated and assembled in a series of images. Entire movies are made on the computer. The *Titanic* sinks; parts are taken out of a model from the classic photo process. Then everything is reworked on the computer. These things would have been unthinkable even three years ago. You suddenly notice the interplay of the various software developers.

It does not help when we only have people who are trained in the object-oriented algorithm; now I need engineers who in fact have mastered object-oriented methodology but also understand what kinds of simulation techniques are really possible. We must actually define an image of the engineer where all that belongs.

Thirty years ago, you could specialize in your studies on high-frequency technology, high-voltage technology, or communications technology, all of which belong to electronics. The image of the information scientist must be drawn much broader because business administration has nothing to do with user interactions, for example. It is concerned with numbers and with theories and it also tries to be mathematical.

SCHEER There have also been such developments in teaching business administration. We have reached the limits of putting things into mathematical terms. Will this broader concept also play a role in setting up the new Institute for Software Engineering, or is it more centered on the field of core information science with a looser connection to the wider environment?

The subject matter of the Hasso Plattner Institute

PLATTNER In Potsdam, we want to provide an engineering course of study in connection with normal information science, one that in fact still lies within the realm of information science but concentrates on large-scale systems. It will be about networks, not only the logical description of an Internet, but also about networks as applications systems. It will further go into various types of graphical data processing because graphical systems are becoming more and more valuable, and I believe that they will get the upper hand. We will have moving simulations everywhere. That is already being done in many places where simulations on the computer can determine whether a certain assemblage can be made. I saw this at VW. To see whether the door fits on a vehicle this way or that, they don't try it with a real door, but instead it is tested on the computer, and then they change the door or the car until the assembly can be made.

Learn to understand the whole

What we want to achieve is that the engineers we educate will have an idea of such job assignments. They should have an understanding of the whole, regardless of where they go and what concentration they choose, and learn that there is a lot more to working as an engineer than having 100 percent of a method at your fingertips.

WENDT Naturally, when you are defining a course of study, you cannot just add in material. You can only add in new materials if you get rid of old material because otherwise the study time is extended and that is not acceptable. There must be a shift in the area of concentration. Certain content that now is taught in the information science must be dropped.

The Hasso Plattner Institute in Potsdam.

PLATTNER Yes, perhaps the engineer is not really the best image, but rather a comparison between a construction engineer and an architect. I see information scientist of today more as a construction engineer, and we want to educate architects. Many things come together there; design is one very essential component, but construction materials are also an essential component. Of course, the architect must also study and understand statics for a building to meet certain fundamental physical requirements. Later, of course, in actually implementing the construction project, he will also need people who have specialized in statics. And he needs many others who have specialized in many other areas. But because he is the only one with this overview, he can exercise his role as architect. That is really what we have in mind. We want to educate architects in the field of software systems technology.

The software engineer is like the architect

WENDT Yes, but I would go another step further. David Parnas, a recognized world expert in the field of software engineering whom I spoke with recently, has said that the instructions in information science today have current research subjects strongly in the foreground. Things are reported, and the listeners encounter knowledge that just the day before yesterday was thought out on someone's desk. It is as though the physicists with the latest particles of elements that have just been discovered are presented in the lectures on theoretical physics. But you must not present these things in educating electrical engineers because the usefulness of this knowledge for developing products is still not recognizable and will come out in perhaps 20 years for the first time.

The necessity of teaching content related to the profession

It would be nice if you could learn everything. It is indeed good to know something about everything, but a course of studies has only a certain number of semester hours and you have to budget them. When we return to the education of system architects, there is really no place for an epic discussion of denotative semantics. Information science could have a three-hour lecture for the whole semester on denotative semantics, but in educating an engineer, in contrast, this subject deserves perhaps 20 minutes and then we are done with it.

SCHEER We will have to change the image of the jobs that we will have here in Germany and in Europe in the future. Hardware developers will probably not be the focus of education in information science any more. Software developers in the narrow sense will also perhaps not be the central figures, but rather the software architects that think in broader terms.

PLATTNER We need them all; we need the combination.

SCHEER Right, we need them all, but the question of the relationship does come up. I mean, at the beginning, the focus was on the hardware for quite a long time and now perhaps is on the software, but in too narrow a field, so that you want to validate the accuracy—even though you definitely know that in 20 years you will not be able to substantiate the correctness of a large-scale system. Here we have the contrast between the field of "proper research" in which researchers feel comfortable and the problems that are not seriously regarded from the research side. But the problems are there and they are important and they define the world.

The distance of information science from practice—an anecdote

WENDT I want to bring in an anecdote here, a story from 20 years ago.

I was sitting in a conference in Amsterdam where the famous Edgar Dijkstra, one of the "high priests" of information science, was giving a lecture. He leaned forward and said, "I am always reprimanded because the examples with which I explain my concepts are so small." And, true, they were always programs that would fit on half a page of letter-size paper; sometimes they were only five lines long. "I will accept the blame," he continued, "and today bring you a very complex example from the practical side. I will show you that I also know my way around in reality very well." And then he brought out a program that was two letter-size pages long! I nudged my neighbor in the conference hall and told him that where I worked, program printouts were moved around on a dolly. We were not talking about two letter-size pages, but more than 40,000 letter-size pages, and that is a whole different category. This showed me the main problem in information science.

PLATTNER Another thought occurs to me at this time. We have believed for all too long that it was actually the task of the business administrator or the business administration information scientists to do all this. They plan the system, and then the information scientists are the people who physically implement it. I believe that constructing large systems is a long way beyond what business administrators do. It is clear that part of what you implement is business administration systems, but this construction of the system is something else; it is an independent activity that is also learned, exercised, and practiced as its own discipline.

System development as a separate task and discipline

SCHEER Now we can talk about the conventional labels. Business information science in Germany at least has the merit of noting reality and not being afraid to take on the questions that come up in it, whereas those information scientists who come strongly from the mathematical side have shied away from them. I would even say, looking back at the scanty resources that have been allocated to business information science in Germany, that it deserves a lot of credit.

But in general, systems development is more comprehensive than can be covered by any one specialty discipline, in this case business information science. This is also true for medical systems and applies in exactly the same way for technical systems; that is, we already have an abstraction of it when we ask ourselves how we can assert control over large-scale systems, whether they are business administration systems or others.

PLATTNER Yes, and the world is changing. New disciplines will always develop from the traditional disciplines and split off from them, as in process engineering. In the 60s, Karlsruhe had one of the newest institutes for process engineering, which had broken off from mechanical engineering. Chemical engineering is not a matter of levers and flasks, but rather one of pumps and condensers and other interesting things. There was mechanical engineering long before there was aircraft technology. A whole swarm of new disciplines developed because we are building airplanes. We are now seeing one such development here, and we have to develop the supply side of it. If you study aircraft technology in a targeted way rather than study mechanical engineering, then you can build airplanes more easily than if you had only studied mechanical engineering.

Information science knows nothing about systems like R/3

WENDT I believe, however, that information science lags far behind when you compare it with process engineering, mechanical engineering, and aircraft engineering because process engineering or aircraft engineering are functional areas in which the mechanical engineer builds machines for some kind of purpose. One is building an airplane that must fly, and another is building an entire chemical installation to produce ammonia. We must ask what the process engineer and the aircraft builder have in common. The commonality is actually the common language and the standardized means of description for a large-scale system. The mechanical drawing is not something that you learn for process engineering or for airplane construction, but you learn it because you are building mechanical systems that consist of mechanical construction parts. It does not matter whether it is a pipe through which ammonia flows or the lines in an airplane through which the hydraulic oil flows. The way and manner in which engineers talk about their systems in mechanical engineering is basically predetermined. In information science, you learn practically nothing at all about how to talk about a system like R/3 or any other complex system. The problem lies here.

SCHEER Now we are on the subject of modeling.

The use of modeling

WENDT Indeed. And this modeling will be one of the central tasks of the new Hasso Plattner Institute.

SCHEER Modeling is, on one hand, important as the language of engineers and, on the other hand, as the language you use to communicate with customers. The architect in building construction uses his drawings to talk to his statics man, his suppliers, and those working the trades. He takes the same drawings when he speaks with his customers or those assigning him the task, who have not studied architecture and are not from the trades.

PLATTNER And thus you have defined where we need modeling in dealing with the customers: anywhere that changes should be made, as otherwise we would not be able to talk with each other at all. No one shows me drawings of how an automobile works; I just sit down in the car, turn the ignition key, and drive off.

SCHEER You only get the auto catalog that shows the options and functions you can choose. You see the choice of colors, the various options combinations, and so on.

PLATTNER In the field of automobiles, the variability is very small, in construction it is somewhat larger, and with software, the way we do it, in particular with the New Dimension field described earlier, it is much greater. We therefore are making efforts everywhere to find a form of description that is suitable for various levels of people in showing them just exactly what we do. This is needed so that we can speak with each other and not simply send concepts back and forth without understanding just what we are talking about. The solution map is one form of depiction. It is very important we find a common language that makes it possible to communicate between the various participants. The form of presentation that should show how the components of a software system communicate internally is totally different from the form of presentation that helps us to talk with our customers when selecting the process parameters.

SCHEER We are a long way from reaching the boundaries of imagination. Why should we not pursue virtual reality approaches as is done in architecture? You can explore a building even before it is built and wander around in it at the virtual level. Why should we not be able to move through a business process that goes through several partners within a logistics chain?

Explore the potential for the use of applications

PLATTNER I also consider it very important that the applications in engineering science or the film industry be studied in terms of their potential for reuse. The very expensive systems are virtual reality systems, for crash tests and such things, where the entire physics are included behind them. But you can also partly reuse such programs in very simple commercial applications in the future. Computer performance will grow and grow and grow. There is no indication that computer speed development will somehow stop. It will continue like this for some time to come. We can reuse more of the software that we have created in the last 10 years in other fields as well, and I consider it important that we find out early where the potential lies.

We can use a lot to simplify the system operations. Stop and think about tuning a television set. Nobody today takes a screwdriver to a variable resistor. The trimmer that once stuck out from all television sets—can you still remember it? There were holes in the cabinet housing, so I naturally stuck a screwdriver in there and tried to improve the picture. Now a small component sets the convergence by itself, and when that is not enough, you have an extra operating instruction for interaction with the television itself, as with the computer.

Everything is developing in this direction. Before all other things, 3D will have an influence on our systems.

SCHEER Can we say that software development in the future will be driven more by organizational considerations than by the functional considerations that have prevailed until now? We brought the functions into the program; a statement is nothing other than the conversion of a function. Then we very strongly emphasized the data viewpoint with the data bank architectures. Now we are actually looking at the organization. We look at the role of the user, which is an organizational description. We classify. Until now, we only looked at the organization overall. We have the user, but that is just something gray, the abstract user, the abstract enterprise. Now we must approach these elements more specifically.

What determines future software development?

PLATTNER Well, I would say that the function and the functional further development will remain in the same proportion that they are today.

SCHEER Yes, but an account description is an account description. There will not be any big dynamic development there.

PLATTNER Yes, there will because billing is changing greatly since it comes from all possible angles. An example is transaction-dependent billing in the Internet field. There are already large changes there.

SCHEER Other things come in here as well, such as the classification of billing into certain groups. It is not a matter of the billing itself where I write in a few numbers and add the value-added tax to them.

PLATTNER We are building a huge new invoicing system, a billing system. We have learned a lot from the field of telecommunications, the Internet, and so on. The functional requirements will not become any less essential. It would be wrong to believe that we have arrived and now everything will stay the same. The functionality will probably grow disproportionately. But in addition, and this is the essential point, totally new requirements will arise. This entire user-centered way of looking at things brings an additional aspect.

The dynamics in the organization of the business

SCHEER It is not just changing at the user level, as the organization of the business itself is becoming more dynamic. I now have certain functions in various outside positions, and I have to reconfigure the system to accommodate this organization. The entire distribution is in fact an organizational problem. What will I do where, what data will be kept and which functions provided, what data will I have to use in which functions. It is different in the factory than it is in the sales office. I suddenly am looking closely at the overall organizational diversity. I no longer have one enterprise, one user type, but I have totally different elements. I perhaps retrieve the distributed organizational descriptions from the system itself. A large part of the organizational descriptions were traditionally always in the HR (Human Resources) system, even though they did not belong there. Why would the organization chart of an enterprise be kept in the HR system?

The central problem: the distribution of information

PLATTNER Let's jump back to the applications for a minute. One of the central problems with our current applications is the distribution. Whether we want to reach an employee in sales or the service technician, it is a software distribution problem, a data distribution problem. How do we get certain amounts of data to the PCs of the people who are working in the front lines? How do we get the content they are interested to them, and how do we provide this content to them? With the so-called push and pull development, you distinguish between sending pointers back and forth that only create the possibility of a person acquiring the right information and sending certain information to the technician or the salesman that they can process to find the workload for the next day, the next week, or the next month.

There are a great number of developments, and the distribution mechanisms along the organizational structure of a business stand behind them. It is no longer the case that we have a central headquarters somewhere and perhaps also a post office box.

Recall the old EDP and the boxes you could reach through. The EDP central department would distribute the lists that you printed. They were sorted by name, and you would pass by the other side of the open-ended pigeonholes and retrieve your lists from them. That is what the computer center at SAP looked like 10 or 12 years ago.

I maintain, however, that things are just being added on and nowhere is anything breaking off. When anything does break off at all, it is the proof of value through formal criteria. A date is numerical, but that is really unimportant. You have to know whether the date is allowed in the given context. When the date of a money order matches a bank holiday, then you have an inconsistency. This quality overall is increasing, and there is more semantics being processed. The systems must understand far more information.

WENDT Basically it is a matter of context-dependent semantics. But now I would like to talk about a totally different subject area. We have talked the entire time only about the product and where the functional development of systems is going. We have asked ourselves what will be needed. Because we have Mr. Plattner right at hand, there is something else that greatly interests me, namely how he sees the questions of managing a large company.

When I came to SAP in 1990, it had a thousand employees. Two years later R/3 was delivered. Today SAP has more than 18,000 employees worldwide. That is unbelievable growth of a factor of 18 in 8 years. It therefore would be very interesting to hear from Hasso Plattner, who is in such a responsible position, about what problems he sees there—whether he sees certain procedural methods typical of SAP that are different from, for example, those of IBM, Microsoft, or comparable enterprises. How do you do such things in America, and how do you do them here? Can the success of SAP be traced back essentially to brilliant planning or simply to the utilization of certain evolutionary developments?

The advantages and disadvantages of hierarchies

PLATTNER There certainly isn't any patent on how one best constructs a rapidly growing organization. My colleague also insisted on flat hierarchies and teamwork. I have always said that the reality has long since passed us by, and we have very strong hierarchies. In America, we have up to six levels of hierarchies. Hierarchies mean faster execution, and they mean that you can implement a change in direction and monitor a defined goal.

The hierarchical structure thus has significant advantages: the military-type organization.

It also has, however, the great disadvantage that with all the nodes in the hierarchy, it is very difficult to change some positions. In a hierarchy tree, you cannot move someone down from his current position. You have to come up with special arrangements that set up the same level of hierarchy on the side or insert a level. You end up putting together some unusual arrangements to protect status and protect any employee from losing face. If someone has been vice-president, I cannot suddenly make him a director. That is impossible without having employees leave the business. For an organization of our kind, which is constantly changing and must remain flexible, this causes really big problems.

Not a uniform organization

We do not have any uniform organization throughout. Sales and service can be organized in one way, and development can be organized totally differently. Now, as before, development at SAP is set up so that even members of the board are personally active in development. Of the five members of the board we have today, four are active in development.

SCHEER Do you know of a comparable business where it is similar to this?

PLATTNER Yes, Oracle, at least halfway. Larry Ellison is significantly more active in development than in PR. At Microsoft, Bill Gates just said that Herbold and Ballmer should take care of the implementation in the enterprise so that he can do more for development again. Our development is also something quite extraordinary. Such a large system must have representation on the board for the specialties. We are trying not to become stratified into hierarchies. The hierarchies are the fault lines along which we have difficulties. To build hierarchies is to build points around which people circle the wagons so they can define their tasks themselves. We spoke earlier about how rapidly software is changing. The organizational structures must constantly change along with it, and this is very difficult to achieve.

The best thing that we have at SAP is a culture that we built up over the years and still maintain today. It is really this culture that moves the enterprise forward, and the first characteristic of this culture is honesty. At SAP, you do not get away with lying or with declaring that you have done something or that you can do something that does not jibe with the facts. Everything is examined. If an employee discovers a Potemkin village, you have already lost. It is very difficult to defend a Potemkin village at SAP because everyone has the same opinion that there should not be any. Everyone works to make sure such villages cannot be erected.

The best thing about SAP is the enterprise culture

We look at areas where something is constantly being developed but has no relationship to reality; that is, it will never have any effect on the product. Such areas rapidly crystallize out, and the company builds a cocoon around them. Thereafter it is a management decision about whether this area will be allowed to exist any further. Everyone who comes in new to us notices this culture and also tells us that. The openness of the people and how they deal with each other, how

Openness

they work with each other across the organizational lines, is conspicuous. When I discuss things with people, they can deal with me as if I were a software developer that had just been hired one or two years ago.

A small side issue that is unusual for a German company: Henning Kagermann and I have introduced the practice that people in the company worldwide call us by our first names. All the English-speaking people do it anyway and our language is half English, half German; in contact with the customers, it is more English and within the company it is more German. To avoid talking in different ways, we decided that everyone would call us by our first names. This is the form of address as it should be; I cannot prevent it that many still address me with my title, but this will slowly die out.

The sole reason for this is that we want to take down the barriers. When we have something to do with other companies, they often come with their entire hierarchy, and they are quite confused when we don't show up with this same hierarchy and SAP leaves out three hierarchical levels. We have pursued this idea from the beginning, and now it is written down in the management books. This is naturally not an idea that you can define and then make it reality, but rather you have to keep working at it and fighting for it.

Direct control and direct communications

Let us take, for example, the development meeting I participated in recently. The gentlemen presented what they were doing now and how they wanted to proceed further. They said that they had to work four more weeks on the matter at hand, and then they would submit it to me and the board or I could make a decision. Then I said, "No, we will not do it that way. In a matter of minutes, I can determine what I find good in what you have done so far." We had a 100 percent agreement on which option that the team proposed was the best. I said, "This is the best. Now give me a progress report every week to look at. When I have something to say about it, I will check in, and when I don't say anything, keep right on going. We are working toward an objective, and I can now and then get involved to give direction. But you are not building something that you will show me for the first time at a certain decision point, at which I might change the direction and then we would have to start all over. We will pursue this point, and meanwhile you can keep me informed."

I can thus have an influence on a project and not wait until the meeting at the end when I only have two alternatives between which I must choose. It is somewhat more demanding to influence the development while it is in progress. It requires more communication, but however you set it up, this method of doing things leads to better results.

SCHEER I don't know if it was intentional or not, but you just gave a very precise description from organizational theory about how one can resolve certain problems of coordination. You can work through directives, which is the hierarchical principle. This is not at all a bad way. It functions well in some environments, namely when the task assignments are repetitive. Then an organizational entity functions as a machine. It always produces the same product.

It does not work any longer, however, with very complex tasks that are constantly changing. You can only organize these in terms that also change over time. And, unfortunately, there is no simple principle as that of hierarchical organization. These teams have to steer themselves, and that actually works only through such fuzzy concepts as the culture of the enterprise. If you do not have this, such team organization will not work. This is a prerequisite for such a looser structure.

PLATTNER I would like to bring up another example. We have already played this through a few times in the board and also in the expanded board. It sounds like a truism but actually is rarely put into practice. We discuss a matter and decide upon it only when beforehand all

A principle: find the facts and evaluate them

the facts that pertain to the subject are clear and a consensus on these facts has been reached by all the participants. It almost always goes wrong when you talk about something when only the person making the presentation knows the pertinent facts. The subject could be, for example, setting prices, a market development, or the question of what we can do in UNIX or NT. Then the presenter can declare that we would have to make a decision in favor of UNIX because this or that could not be done in NT. This has occasionally happened with us in the past.

When only the presenter knows the facts, the others can do nothing other than demand proof and say, "We first must see whether the facts agree and we must now discuss the facts." Then someone says that we must make a decision in order to stick to the schedule. "We have to come to a decision." And I say, "Damn, this is not the way it goes. I will not make any decision

The SAP board at the time with the supervisory board chairman Dietmar Hopp (third from left): Claus E. Heinrich, Henning Kagermann, Peter Zencke, Gerhard Oswald, and Hasso Plattner (from left to right).

when I am in doubt about the facts." Peter Zencke says, "Well, you cannot count on me. If I do not know the facts, or when I cannot grasp them or when they do not agree, it does not work. And then I cannot make any contribution and therefore abstain."

This is how we work, and it is difficult. It leads to a savings of time when we must determine the facts beforehand. They are cleared up bilaterally in advance. If someone comes to a conference and says that he did not have the time to check the facts, he really has to abstain. No matter how clever I am or how rapidly I can look through things to see whether something might not agree, I must abstain because I have not prepared myself beforehand.

This method is supported by help from the staff members because you cannot do everything personally. But with this method, we can get along with each other in meetings significantly more harmoniously. If someone does not bring in the facts or has failed to familiarize himself with them, he should not get engaged and he can allow himself only very cautiously to join in the discussions. Through this preparation and getting all the facts, almost all the participants have already reached a decision in their minds. The decision-making process takes its course, and we come more or less simultaneously to the same result. I will bring up here the ages-old example, which is a classic one for me.

In the beginning years of R/2, around 1981, we constantly had problems with the memory. The memory would get full, and we had problems with freeing up the memory, garbage collection problems. Every morning we would have a meeting when a problem turned up for a customer. We no sooner had resolved it in MVS than it would not work in DOS. We no sooner had resolved it in DOS than it would not work in BS 2000. At that time, we had a component that we would immediately exchange live so that we always got feedback when something was not working.

Example: the memory problem in the R/2

One evening we were talking, and all the employees who were involved were present. I said, "We cannot go on like this." The answer was, "Yeah, the world is so complicated." My question was, "Tell me, just what is the problem here?" The answer was, "It stems from the fact that we are connecting four different operating systems to one piece of software simultaneously, and this does not work." Question, "Tell me, why are there actually four different operating systems?" Answer, "DOS, MVS, BS 1, and BS 2." Question, "Did you say BS 1? How many installations do we have on BS 1?" Answer, "Two, and one of these is going over to BS 2." Question, "Why don't we just take BS 1 totally out of it?" Answer, "That would be no problem."

We had been tormenting ourselves, along with the customer, because the garbage collection caused errors. The system would stop and crash, red lights would come on, and it would be fixed over the telephone. This had been going on for at least six months in this conversion phase of R/2, and the best people we had always had to fix it.

SCHEER But a marketing thought had occurred to the developer, and previously it was all the same to him whether it was 1 or 1,000 systems, he didn't care.

Example: the data bank does not perform

PLATTNER This is just what I mean about finding out the facts and evaluating the facts. I simply took out the fact that we also had to solve the problem for the BS 1, and the equation could immediately be solved. When we have problems that we currently cannot solve, I always try to think in this direction, whether we do not have to change the evaluation of the facts. We should not immediately give up just because we do not believe something and say that we cannot do it.

For example: "The data bank cannot work up to performance requirements." Then I ask, "Wait a minute, what performance are we thinking about here?" Answer, "Well, for any number of users." Question, "Wait a minute, how many users do we have for this application at Boehringer in Mannheim?" Answer, "I don't know." Question, "How many do we have at SAP then?" Answer, "I don't know that either." "Then we must first find out the facts and determine just how many users we actually have who are accessing the common data bank. Before we do that, we cannot meaningfully discuss the problem. With one user, we have no blockage problem, and with two users only a very small one. Do we perhaps have 50 users or 500 or 5,000?" "There can't be, since we seldom have such a large-scale system with so many active users. With 50 users, I can imagine that it would work alright." Then I say, "Thank you. We must not let ourselves be misled and not utilize a certain system technology just because it does not work with really big numbers of users. It is enough that it works with small numbers of users as we have here." We get away from this abstract equation that tries to solve everything.

I really do imagine this in terms of equations. If the original equation was that it had to perform with 1 up

Teamwork at SAP in Walldorf.

to 50,000 or up to infinity users, then I can return to the equation and say it is enough for it to perform with 1 to 50 users. I could also have an equation with the determination that SAP can never program in Java. I can take this out of the equation: "We can also program in Java, but we must not program only in Java." So we must understand each other, what we mean, precisely beforehand. Otherwise, it can easily happen that we will argue again and again about, for example, whether Java will never work. I consider this a completely wrong path, and you can easily lose the fact-based foundation and become polemic.

SCHEER That is in principle the difference between fundamentalists and realists. The one can only decide between 0 and 1, and the other knows that there is also something between them.

Motivation through joy in the work

PLATTNER The method of proceeding just described works with the board very well, and we try to promote it in the rest of the organization as well. The lower teams work this way in any case. This is really the good thing about teamwork at SAP; the work occurs in teams without thought of careers or hierarchies. The career is that you have fun with the development of a great product in a good business and that you get paid more based on performance. It is therefore very dangerous to introduce hierarchical compensation models. We must fight these models with a countering movement because otherwise they lead to building hierarchies. We introduced an earnings system with 15 steps, and that is an implicit hierarchy. It is more of a problem than a help. It is truly a problem when people think in terms of these levels instead of thinking of doing what makes them happy.

I believe that a very essential aspect of why SAP works so well despite the high number of employees is that the work is fun. We have only a 2 percent employee turnover in Walldorf. The people enjoy working here. This was also shown in an opinion poll. In America, we have a significantly higher turnover. In America, many people come to SAP because they want to earn money. They also have fun, but then they leave the company again because they go someplace else where they can make even more money and still have fun. These connections to the enterprise come not from pure loyalty, but rather many people work here because they enjoy working together with others whom they value intellectually. That is a very essential component here at SAP, that the people value and respect each other intellectually and enjoy working together.

SCHEER Where are the opportunities of the German software industry? Could there be another SAP in Germany or in Europe? Or was this a unique case determined by certain people who had the same idea coming together and encountering a certain market situation? Or can one prepare the ground for new developments in similar or other areas through targeted educational and research initiatives, as you are trying with your institute?

The chances of a European software business

SAP is indeed a special case because, both before and after, 80 to 90 percent of the software in the world comes out of America, and we here in Europe have only two or three big enterprises that can call themselves global. How do you assess the development in Europe and in Germany? We have seen that we are not all that far behind in research. I am asked by colleagues from America, from MIT or elsewhere, about the architecture of the R/3 system because they have no experience at all in that country with such a thing. Despite this, America has created this great authority on software.

PLATTNER First of all, it was not SAP alone that appeared at this time, but there was an entire forest of software publishers, and we are the tree that grew the strongest. For a long time, SAP was far from number one in Germany. There was SCS, there was ADV Orga, and at the time, there were already Steeb and Strässle, IBM and Kienzle, Siemens and Nixdorf. There were many software companies, and SAP pulled out in front in a

America as the gateway to the world market

certain field, in this ERP field and especially in the field of finance for service enterprises, and then conquered the world.

We did not conquer the world because it had called out to us, but rather because we had clearly planned that we would have to go to America and that we had to be successful in America. Anyone who is not successful in America will also not be successful in the rest of the world. It was a very clear strategy that we carried out rapidly and energetically. The big transition from R/2 to R/3, from mainframe to client/server, stopped us in the middle of this strategy after 55 R/2 installations, and there was a short jolt. Now we have more than 5,000 R/3 installations in America.

Scheer Everyone has memories like that. I remember that in the discussion about America, yes or no, SAP was at the beginning rather hesitant or careful.

Plattner Not hesitant, but yes, careful.

Scheer Some people said that we would rather let ourselves be brought in by customers than enter aggressively.

Let yourself be brought in by customers

Plattner We said: We must be attractive for the American customers. We will not do it in America as America would perhaps do it in Europe. They would advertise and then wait for the jobs. We let ourselves be brought over there by the customers. Very clearly. Mobil, DuPont, Dow Chemical, ICI, those were the first ones; the chemical and oil industries brought us over to America. In the PC industry, at first there were a lot, Ashton-Tate, Borland. For a long time, Lotus was the biggest enterprise and then Microsoft. Microsoft developed, and the others did not get along so well. Now there are a lot of other software publishers. There certainly will be one or more among them that will take a similar path to that of SAP in which they grow significantly stronger than their competition. I cannot say now in what field this will be or what software it will be. If you could predict that, playing the market would be simple.

I believe that the chances for software companies in Europe are good if they take to heart that it is a global market and that you have to be successful in America. Almost everyone who is now successfully doing software in Europe has set up a branch in America and goes either to California or to the East Coast. Where we have taken the lead is the essential contribution of SAP to this story that you can be successful as a software publisher in Europe over the long haul if you go to America. We make 40 percent of our global profit in America and 20 percent in Germany. It was certainly a difficult process and certainly also a bit of a culture shock. Now we really are a global company, and we also have to live with the fact that the Americans think differently about many things than we do. We should not belittle this and make jokes about it, but rather must take it seriously.

We should, however, always appreciate the capable people we have here in Germany, for example, that we do not constantly change businesses and that we also do not have to make business cards longer to get the titles on them. We need less of this here. I believe that we have good opportunities in Europe, but you must participate in this internationalization and you must go to America, the biggest domestic market. England and the English language alone are not enough. The English software publishers show this as well, and they are located in England and have no linguistic or cultural problems. Without a sufficient presence in the US, they have no chance. Baan did it right, even though they did a lot of other things wrong.

Capable Germans prove their worth

SCHEER We have been speaking about the entry into America. There was the R/3 announcement in the US. I was at SAPPHIRE at the time when you said, "You can buy R/3 now." That was a decision that had been made overnight. Klaus-Dieter Leidig told me that he sat next

The decision: going to America with the R/3

to you in the airplane on the flight to America and that he said, "I have to go back home to my parent group, and I have to tell them about my great cooperative work with SAP. Unfortunately, you do not run on our HP computers." At the time, you were mainframe oriented with the R/2. So the decision was made overnight to announce that R/3 was available in America, to the horror of the American SAP organization.

PLATTNER It was a little different from that. The system already ran on the HP. In 1990, I believe, HP came and said to the developers that they should order a couple of computers. Then they tried to get through to SAP or me through various channels and I said, "Your computers are too slow, and we could hardly use them." Then we used them as terminals, very expensive terminals. These were the CAD systems from HP and were not so well liked because they produced tremendous amounts of heat and could not stand up to a comparison with the DEC workstations at that time. They were the thing to have at the time. And then came the break. At one of the Hannover Fairs, I said that we had

First general meeting of SAP AG (May 1990) with Dietmar Hopp at the speaker's lectern.

already purchased the HP machines and we were running on the HP. But back to the story about America.

In the fall of 1992, we wanted to sell 200 R/3 systems. We had already reached about 130. We could achieve 200 in 1992, but they would not bring in enough money. The income in the mainframe area was dropping at the time. SAP was already on the stock market. So Dietmar and I sat down together and thought about what we could do. I pled the case of increasing R/3 turnover. He threw in that we would cause a shutdown in the income from R/2 with the increase in income from the R/3 area in Germany. We agreed that he should continue to promote the R/2 system in Germany and accept that the R/3 income in Germany would look worse because of this.

For a long time, Dietmar Hopp kept the banner of the mainframe waving high with statements like R/3 does not perform, it does not run on the right computers, and the mainframe will not become extinct. The German customers also saw it the same way. We did not say anything to the contrary and we did not make them insecure. In Germany, people believed that this was the right way. The Americans with their delight in technology were convinced that the mainframe was dead. Everyone was writing about the death of the mainframe.

The dual strategy: R/2 and R/3

In a countermove, we therefore announced the R/3 in America. On January 1, 1993, the product release was supposed to happen in any case. Then on September 15, 1992, I said, "The R/3 is here and whoever orders it now will receive it in six weeks. If there is anything wrong in the translation, since it was supposed to be ready on January 1, we will fix it within six weeks. And if that is not good enough, you will receive a translator delivered free." That was approximately my original text.

The Americans heard that R/3 was there. We unveiled the system on an HP machine with great celebration. The English translation was still somewhat clumsy, but

"The glass is half full"

we still had six weeks left. And the press wrote that R/3 was there and had come a quarter-year early. Only later did the Americans discover that I had chosen an American form of presentation, that of "Half full, not half empty." When they say, "We will come late in the first quarter," that means the second quarter. Simple to create a positive effect with a different verbal presentation. Right at SAPPHIRE, someone bought the first R/3, and by the year's end we had sold 10 R/3 systems in America.

Leadership style

SCHEER We spoke previously about the importance of teams and about the disadvantages of a hierarchy. Despite this, you must at certain times act on the business in a way to give it direction. We discussed here the isolated cases, for example, the transition from R/2 to R/3, where you had to find a solution very rapidly under pressure of time and make a decision about how it would run in America. You announced the solution yourself there, even though the offices in Philadelphia groaned about it. They had just built up half of the R/2 know-how there, and they had to switch over to R/3. But it had to happen!

PLATTNER Yes, our American business had to convert thoroughly. At the time, it was Klaus Besier who had to switch within four weeks from the approach "We will try out R/3 for a while in California" to "We will sell R/3 throughout America." It was quite a shock for them because it came unannounced, and nobody but Dietmar Hopp and I, as well as the others who flew with us to America, knew about this. We had advanced R/3 three months in the minds of the public. But it was just a brief shock, and they signed on to it immediately and acted in a successful way. The golden years of 100 percent growth began then.

SCHEER How do you handle this apparent contradiction that you want a consensus within the team and do not want a hierarchy, but still want the authority to put the helm hard over from the left to the right?

PLATTNER Well, we did the whole thing in SAP through financial control. SAP has always known very specifically what the numbers are. It is to Dietmar's credit that SAP has always had a very clear idea of what the profit is, how much we can spend, and how much we can invest. We have often done a project when we have not known how long it would take, particularly the R/3 project. It took far longer than planned. Nonetheless, during this project we made sure that the business was in good shape financially.

Leading through indicators

What do we do today? We are doing a lot today with benchmarking. Information must be presented in the same or similar formats, whether it is the market potential or the developments in the market. They must all be reported in certain patterns, even though the patterns are constantly changing. Our territories must all report to us in one pattern. We take the cost of this upon ourselves.

The first statement of financial position at a press conference (May 1990) with SAP chief of finances Dieter Matheis, Hans-Werner Hector (hidden), Klaus E. Tschira, Hasso Plattner, and Dietmar Hopp (from left to right).

This control through these reporting formats is strongly based on facts so that it is not always just personal. "You are showing only 10 percent growth, so off with your head." There is a lot more fact finding done through these reporting formats. In accordance with these numbers, there is very tight control through performance targets. We are also doing this for development, and this will not be easy. We are now planning what the IBUs will want to have, and development is planning what we can deliver. And there is, of course, a big discrepancy between the two. The overlap is almost zero. We must reach an agreement through a multilevel reconciliation process.

Fact finding as a corrective measure

I believe that we always come back to this recognition that we can improve on complex decision-making only by improving on the prior fact finding. We cannot improve them through cleverness, through power, or through brilliance. For example, SAP South Africa had the idea, "We are done with the idea that SAP always says we will not do any end-user training. We must do end-user training with the businesses." They are therefore developing a role-based training program together with Andersen Consulting, and now the whole world is saying, "Wonderful, we have been waiting for this for so long."

We can also suddenly develop something totally new, and that must cut through all the plans and go against the budget considerations. On the board, we try to take both these paths, but you cannot continually say, now I have a degree of freedom and therefore my numbers are bad, or vice versa. One half of the brain must be thinking in numbers, facts, budget, and schedules, and the other half of the brain must think, "If we continue to go this way, we will never reach the goal; somehow there must be an idea about how we can do this different and better. This goes against the current planning, but in the end, it will improve the numbers."

Dietmar Hopp and I have used this method of proceeding for a long time now. As it has been reported over and over again, it was not that Dietmar was the man in charge of finances and that I did the software. Dietmar has done as much programming as I have, and he has sold just as much as I have sold. In one year, 1974, he even sold more than I did, which really stunk as far as I was concerned. I had a couple of prospects who did not come in by Christmas. That was a sad Christmas celebration. I believe it was 1975.

WENDT SAP has been connected with certain names in the past, like Plattner and Hopp, who have made a large contribution to its success. For me, it is an interesting question how a company that grows as much as SAP brings along its next generation of leadership. Whom do you send to management training, and how is he selected? Are there suddenly such concepts as "middle-management levels" or "upper-management levels," and is there a pool of potential leadership personnel?

PLATTNER I will not say anything against it. I believe that this is the most important thing—and I believe that this is also the decisive factor in the success of Microsoft: to have good people in the top positions of SAP who also look so attractive to those on the outside that we get new people through them. The ones we want to recruit are those who enjoy working with our top people. The employees who leave SAP must be sad that they are losing something. We have already had people leave and send me letters in which they write that they enjoyed working here and that it distresses them to be somewhere else and to have left, but that they had to pursue their life plans in another direction. That keeps us together. That shows those being hired that it is attractive to work for this enterprise.

How do you get good employees?

You do not come to SAP as a public assistance facility where you get a meal for free. I hope fewer than 10 percent come to us for reasons of money. You come to SAP because, for example, it is a pleasure to work with Henning Kagermann, because you meet with clear ideas, and because there is a great style in the development. Employees are not molded into a form, sliced up, and then put back together. Elsewhere, one says, "I am an IBMer, or I am a Procter & Gambler man, or now I am an Arthur Andersen man." With us, an employee very much keeps the personality he has. We are not into forming personalities at SAP.

SCHEER Yes, but sometimes you are asked by journalists who think you have insider information. These journalists sometimes have doubts in reporting on SAP boards because they do not fit the stereotypes.

PLATTNER Thank God!

SCHEER So a journalist says, "I don't know what I should say because he doesn't fit the image I have of a manager at all."

The SAP style: lead through persuasion

PLATTNER For example, SAP does not function with "threatening and fear." SAP does not work this way, even though I use it now and then. Dietmar has always said that people are afraid of me, and I reply, "No, they are afraid of you." A few certainly are afraid, but that is not my style, to create fear, but rather to persuade. When I cannot convince an employee I am right, then I look for the fault in myself. It is my incapability to persuade them. And when they have become too stubborn or inflexible, it is my responsibility that they have become that way. I should have taken steps earlier to keep them more flexible. Now you have to work on the matter. I believe that practically all the employees of SAP have more or less this understanding.

Naturally, it is not propagated everywhere that this is our style. When new employees who are quite different come into the business, they do not fit in at SAP. Many Americans have difficulties at SAP because they need this "law and order," this clear hierarchy, the directives, the production targets, and the fulfillment that a bonus brings with it. They see it is not that way at SAP.

Despite our size, I believe that this is still our most valuable plus. Naturally, we talk every day about how

In front of the main entrance to the DSC (development and sales center).

difficult it is to control the structure and to keep the motivation high.

Now we are implementing the initiative EnjoySAP. Yesterday we had 450 employees there when Mr. Esslinger of Frog Design gave a lecture. They were hanging on his every word. Afterwards, I looked at the new design with him, and I said, "Man, that looks a whole lot better. It is fun again to do software. We are renewing ourselves again, but through a group dynamic."

Certainly I have to take on the project and lend a hand, but I have already said that I am not taking it on my shoulders, but always delegate it downward. The joy must be way down there by the developers and no different with our users.

A hearty welcome to the employee party for the 25th anniversary of the company in 1997.

Recognize the right thing and do it unflinchingly

In many books you can read that the employee is the most important thing, and so on, but you also have to do something about it. And SAP has, I believe, done better than some other businesses. Part of it is that Mr. Plattner is also working and not off sunning himself somewhere or presenting himself as a royal monarch. It is hard enough to reach me. I work less than I did 20 years ago, and the enterprise has grown 40-fold. So I have relatively less time for one individual. Naturally, that is a problem, but we do not let ourselves be steered by some management cookbook or the *Harvard Business Review*. Dietmar Hopp has always said this as well. Many things we have done in management we would today describe with statements like, "Actually you had to do it exactly like that, and you had to organize yourself exactly like that." SAP is not perfect, but it is still a great business.

Chapter 5

Seize the Initiative: mySAP.com

We are making totally new processes and that is the difference. We make totally different demands on the employees, in part very dramatic ones. On one hand, we want to show imagination, and on the other hand, we want to do this in a multifaceted way—both, and that is a difficult task. And I believe it is a task that only such an enterprise as SAP could perform.

Walldorf, August 24, 1999

SCHEER I recently read an article that raised the question whether ERP systems have become superfluous because of the new Internet applications. Is a functioning ERP system a prerequisite for e-commerce applications? Will the ERP system then be the backbone system on which you can flesh out the e-commerce systems, or can you say that ERP systems have come to a total collapse?

PLATTNER I have never liked the term ERP (Enterprise Resource Planning). I believe that it was coined by the Gartner Group. We developed our systems more as operational than as planning systems and thereby developed enterprise development systems for all possible business processes. Only in the last few years have we moved more strongly into planning. When we developed R/3, you said at a supervisory board meeting that we should not build a production system of the old type and that we must orient ourselves toward modern production methods. We had also seen then in America that production had changed. There are more and more businesses that do only the design, the sales, and the service. At best, there will also be a pre-production workshop that builds the prototypes. The rest of the production is outsourced to Asia or somewhere else. The production then happens there.

The Internet changes the way businesses work together

We had to learn that production has changed in the last 10 to 15 years. What is now changing, however, is the way and method that businesses work together overall, that they are permanently connected with each other in a simple manner and not only with a high-speed line, as between the big automobile manufacturer and his 10 biggest suppliers. Practically everyone is connected with everyone else. New potential is created by this.

Example: procurement over the Internet

Let us take, for example, our B2B procurement. This development is just 12 months old and supports purchasing over the Internet. The first thing is to build up a catalog and to find and indicate the businesses on the Internet. Additionally, procurement development over the Internet is supported but strongly driven from the purchasing system. We have gone a step further and said to ourselves, "Why not go on to the selling system? Let's make the selling system an active system, just as we work manually. When we go to buy something on the Internet, let's access the selling system to put together a product configuration." We thus use the seller's software to bring the end result into our business. This is exactly what we do with our B2B procurement. We go on to the selling system and, through an agreement with the manufacturer or the operator of the selling system, we take over the total result of the activity in the form of XML messages and then feed it into our enterprise accounting system.

From the viewpoint of the purchasing enterprise, the purchasing transaction takes place in the seller's system. The budget administration, the release of funds, the verification of authority, whether a person is authorized to buy a PC for 5,000 DM, in contrast take place in our own enterprise system. And such combinations were unthinkable until yesterday for normal commercial systems.

SCHEER If you now try to generalize this and trace it back: We can certainly discuss the term ERP, but it is, in my opinion, a further development of the MRP (Material Requirement Planning) concept, where handling the material in an industrial plant was in the foreground. Then there was MRP II (Manufacturing Resource Planning). This was an expansion to the entire logistics chain, but still related to industry operations. Then we looked for a concept that would reach out further and consider not just the industrial plant, but rather the general enterprise. ERP was developed as a result. The "P" was carried over into this, whether it is meaningful or not. But it was indeed the idea of looking at the entire enterprise and connecting the salesman's applications with the logistics applications.

PLATTNER If we would call the systems the "Enterprise Business Systems," I would feel fine. This would be the opposite of the engineering applications for the design and construction of some things.

SCHEER Or commerce applications that were all already specialized. The next point, about which you have already spoken: Is there a change at this time in the speed at which systems are being further developed or in the way in which we are pursuing this development from the philosophical standpoint? Is the technology alone no longer sufficient to bring forth a new system generation? You took up this thread with R/3—the client/server architecture as technology, but with absorption of the existing concepts along with it. Now we have the Internet as the new technology, and we cannot transfer the old concepts from the organization side into it. The interworking between new organizational forms, how enterprises work with each other, and the new technology are much stronger here and indeed lead to changing both. You must perhaps

What will determine the next system generation?

change the systems from the platform out, and you also need the imagination to develop new applications.

PLATTNER It is much more the latter. The technology has remained more or less the same. Let's just look at R/3; we have always kept the client relatively small. . . .

SCHEER We actually maintained the centralized concept.

R/3 architecture versus Internet technology

PLATTNER And we have always had the three-level client/server architecture in R/3. First we split off the data bank and separated the data from the actual operations and from the presentation. Finally, we split off the presentation, where previously we had prepared the presentation on the applications server where the operations take place. This is exactly the technology of the Internet. This is why it is hard for all the analysts to understand why SAP actually has it so easy in marching onto the Internet. Much easier than, for example, our colleagues at PeopleSoft or at Oracle, who have made their software very client-heavy and now must completely rewrite it. It is relatively easy for us to cope with the even more centralized approach of the Internet. And the approach is centralized because very little functionality is housed at the client and a whole lot at the applications server. The applications server controls several data servers or other servers that I would call "process servers."

Applications that go beyond the system

What is now happening is that an application no longer moves out from the user over several stages to access a data source, but rather it moves in several directions simultaneously. It accesses various data sources. Today we are building applications that relate to execution by various data banks and by various service providers. Let us take, for example, planning a trip or an event. We can lay claim to the services of the transportation business or the airline, as well as the reservations systems of hotels, rental cars, and service personnel. Perhaps we must also use the reservations system of a conference center. It is still a matter of a project within an enterprise. Instead of keeping all the information in the enterprise system, however, we can now use the services directly, and we receive information from the service providers that we can bring directly into our systems. From the user's viewpoint, the entire application takes place for the most part in the service systems of the airlines, the convention center, or the management service providers that organize it overall and then to a lesser extent in his own enterprise business system.

SCHEER Where is the additional value that SAP then provides? Is it in the broker function from the technical side, to provide systems, or does it go beyond this, in that you perhaps construct a trust center?

PLATTNER We started very early in SAP to move the data processing that happened in the background of the enterprise to the front, to bring it to the users. We then transferred more and more of the processes there, where more know-how about the processes is available. We performed services for others in doing so. Auditing was one such nice example. We did the creditor accounting along with the auditing, because auditing the accounts is the most important matter. The developments afterwards, the number-crunching, is really just a mechanical process.

Enterprise business systems are necessary, now as before

Now we have the opportunity once more to take a look at the entire processes anew from the viewpoint of those who must develop them, that is, from a project viewpoint. We must not have an enterprise system that has to be fed with information to create a bill. On the other hand, it will have to be created in the future, as well. And it is therefore a mistake to say that we do not need any business systems in the enterprise any more. We need them now, just as before.

Collaboration

A large part of what goes on does, however, takes place outside the enterprise. Transactions take place between partners with whom you work. The example of the organization of a conference event shows that. The one who takes on the organization of it, who implements the project, has to work together with the team. In the world of the future, we will work together with outside service providers just as we do with the departments in our own enterprise. We will work with the external systems just as we do with our own enterprise system. And we can combine the systems.

mySAP.com—workplace

How do we reach this goal? We are specifically acting on two levels, once at the "marketplace" and then also at a relatively simple level, at the so-called "workplace" portal. We construct menus there that relate not just to one application, but to several applications. This is happening now with the further development of R/3 in mySAP.com by itself. We have the R/3 core applications, the accounting, logistics, and personnel matters, as three separate systems. Then we have the Knowledge Management and Business Warehouse (BW). The strategic enterprise management is built on this. We have the Advanced Planner and Optimizer (APO), and we have the CRM-type applications within it, e-business, buying, and selling. All of these applications are separate entities.

We already have the problem that we must let the user look at several systems simultaneously. He no longer works mainly in one system, but rather he works scattered around over several systems. Now we have to extend the whole thing over the next stage in which he can work not only on the applications provided by SAP, but also in other applications that exist in an enterprise. The next stage is where he also works with the applications available as services on the Internet.

Role-specific menus

What the portal now provides is first of all menu management at the user level, and it is role-specific. So a secretary has a different menu set from a sales manager or a salesman or someone in maintenance service. These role-specific menus exist everywhere. The connections between the individual applications that do

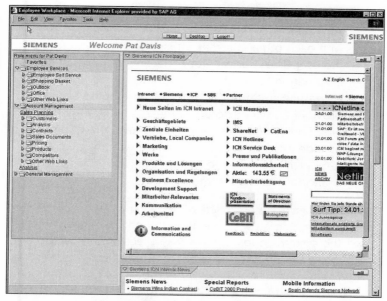

Role-based and personalized mySAP.com workplace.

not know each other can be established in a relatively simple way using an intelligent drag-and-drop level.

To give a simple example for the applications that we are now doing: I buy something over the Internet and the seller tells me it will be shipped by, for example, FedEx. I receive a FedEx shipment number. That is included somewhere in my order. Days later, I want to know where my order is. I call up the order, finding it under the date or under my name, and I find the shipment number in the order. I can pick it up, drag it over, and let it drop on an icon "FedEx." In connection with this, a mini-application starts and drops the shipment number into the Internet application: "Where is the FedEx shipment with this shipment number at this time?" I see the information displayed on the screen that, for example, the freight is at this time at the Atlanta airport and its arrival in San Francisco is planned for tomorrow.

This is already possible today. We can build ourselves such mini-applications and thus connect applications with each other and make it simple and comfortable for the user. The user will not know any more whether the information about the shipment has come from my enterprise system or from the system of the service provider FedEx. It does not make any difference to him. Earlier, you first had to bring all information from outside into the enterprise system. Then you could retrieve it according to your need. Now it has totally changed with the Internet.

I can access the service system or my business partner and immediately obtain information. This means that the system coupling must take place so that we do not integrate information we do not need into a system. For example, the shipment number has only a tempo-rary value for the execution of the transaction. Perhaps I still have to archive the shipment number; I don't

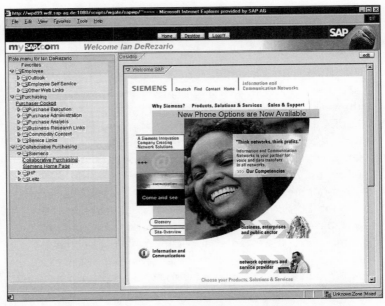

Buying over the Internet on the mySAP.com workplace.

know. But the main value is that the specialist who has to track the order or the purchaser or the engineer can make further plans because he can access the information directly at the service provider.

We now can build the transactions in a new way. This interesting variation leads to the fact that we are implementing much more integration than we have in the past 25 years. It no longer concerns only processing transactions in one enterprise. My examples show in what direction it is going. The processing actually takes place directly on the business partner's side. And now some people say that more and more services will be coming from the Internet.

The transactional world opens up to the Internet

SCHEER SAP started off with commercial applications and grew large with them. An advantage with this was the early connection of the commercial and operational sides of a procedure. That means that when the purchaser put in an order, it was already known in accounting. How do we get this viewpoint in the partner systems as well? Will that lead to a change where we temporarily uncouple the commercial side more strongly than it had been? Will we give up part of the original strength of the conception of this system because you say the commercial side must not pursue such a process—but rather we will first take the operational part and then we will make the interface to this commercial side perhaps more traditional through a batch input, or just how?

PLATTNER This is just what is happening throughout the world. The important thing is bringing this operational side onto the Internet now and using the advantages of the Internet. Today that is the biggest inspiration in America. And the first ones who are successful in this sense, who have installed such systems, have already reached the boundary of frustration, which is "What happens after the transaction? How does the data then get into my billing system?"

Integrating the transaction worlds of the Internet and the enterprise system

Not a single production company in the world does not have a project accounting office. The costs are allocated to the project, to the product, to the cost centers, and then later back to the product. Otherwise I don't have any billing system, I don't have any pricing system, and I really don't have a proper company any more.

The frustration is visible already, and I therefore believe that it must be done differently. We already know a lot about the person who is carrying out the operational activities. We know where he works, what project he is implementing, and what cost center he is assigned to. We can very easily place this person in the organizational hierarchy of the enterprise. With little cost, we can construct an automatic accounting system around this person. From the context in which this person works, we can derive the accounting. The missing account information comes out of the activities. If a product or service is purchased, whether the product is purchased for a project or for warehousing, all this is implicitly contained in the procedure.

If we can embed the actual purchase transaction that takes place on the seller's side into a purchasing transaction that takes place in my company, then I can process the entire account cycle. I thus include the two transaction worlds. I start off to procure something for a project, and I store the actual procurement procedure over the Internet on the page where I am doing the buying. That means that when I come back with the data, I can simply integrate the data in the data set that is already stored in the enterprise system.

SCHEER That means that I obtain the asking price of my supplier myself by accessing the functionality of his system, and then I can actually continue the process as previously.

Price transparency on the Internet **PLATTNER** Yes, and now we see a development. If we stay with the purchasing, you know that prices vary through the Internet. The price transparency of the Internet is perhaps the biggest economic change. At first, it just seems to be the rapid access. You could perhaps have achieved this in some other way as well. We have now achieved it in this way. The immediate consequence is that the prices become transparent. This has happened in the past year in the PC business. Within a few minutes, I can get an overview of where I can get the same performance, probably with the same construction elements, at a better price with better service. Because of this, prices will not be stable for longer periods of time, but rather will fluctuate. Internet auction houses are further intensifying movement in this direction.

This means that an internal catalog at home in which I can buy at this or that price is for many things no longer suitable. It is much better to get the price directly from the seller's page while keeping in mind the existing business relationships to your partners, the volume processed in the past, and the duration of the business relationship. Sales pages are all personalized, and they will appear differently in a company-specific manner and will have a complicated rebate pricing system. This is not buying CDs or books, but rather it is more complicated than that. The sales pages must be adjusted to their customers; they must be like the order processing systems in the enterprises today when they are operated by the usual sales personnel. Now the buyers operate them and serve themselves with this system.

The pressure to let systems work together

I believe that this obligatory price transparency of the Internet also will lead to us having to work like this. The price I got a month ago might already be wrong. I can get a better one. We are experiencing this with special prices on flights. With flights, we are moving in the direction that we will have agreements with the big airlines. We have these already today. We work permanently on the basis of these agreements. They depend on the volume of the turnover made. We try to process the rest at a good price on the spot markets. Both mean that I have to work directly with the other system.

I no longer have the know-how on prices in my system, but rather I have it in the other systems. I have it in the relationship. That is the integration at the next higher level. It is not a matter of building a narrow special system so that it performs well, but the idea is to place this system in a larger context. And I believe that the cooperation between companies will develop in this direction. The next level is to have common plans. The consumer and the producer will come together on the Internet and say, "Let's at least integrate the planning data of our two systems with each other so we will both see an advantage from it."

SCHEER Now the marketplace is more than a technical integration.

PLATTNER We want to let this integration take place on the marketplace, the integration between the systems of the seller, the buyer, the producer, and the distributor.

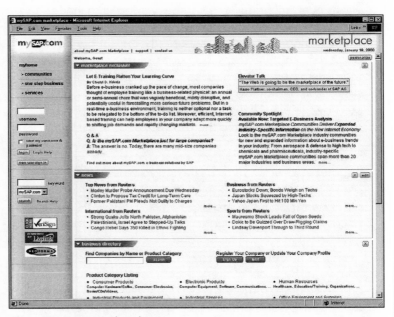

The mySAP.com marketplace.

This integration does not have a 1:1 relationship, but rather an n:m relationship. One sells to many, and one buys from several. Now we have to reduce these many relationships to a few as much as possible. We do this through a so-called converter, and that is the marketplace. The marketplace is the key to how you take the sales information, the end result of the sales process, and transform that into purchasing information. We do this for the selling company, but then everyone who buys over the marketplace can use it. Thus we must do it only once for the company and then everyone can use it.

SCHEER This is practically a kind of EDI.

PLATTNER Yes, there is a standardizing function taking place in the marketplace. If the selling companies also standardize further through these procedures, for example, through industry norms, then we restrict the number of our variants.

SCHEER If the supplying and receiving systems both use this norm, then we avoid the conversion.

PLATTNER That would be wonderful. The next step is not only that I take the results of the order and then send back how the order looks in order to produce the legal document of the contract. The next step is that we get into demand planning and report beforehand that we are planning on the procurement of a certain number of products or services. Can't I take what I already know to plan better, reduce the inventory costs, and reduce the delivery time? For example, I must have a certain quantity of a product in the warehouse to meet the immediate needs. This applies further to the quantity of spare parts stored and so on. At the next level, we go to our customers and see whether they can give us any data so we can work out what he will be ordering in the near future.

The next step: demand planning

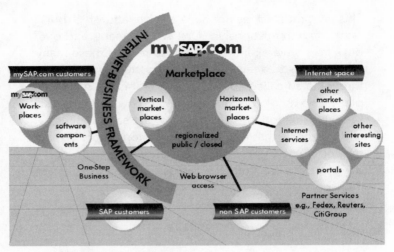

The mySAP.com marketplace concept.

SCHEER This also brings in economies. When you get to this point, information will be substituted for materials. Earlier, in a logistics chain, each individual partner would set up things on the worst case of the others, therefore building up stockpiles, consider how the other would take care of things, and then accordingly add to or draw down from his amount to cover emergencies.

The meaning of logistics

PLATTNER The fact that in 24 hours you can reach practically every spot in the world applies here. In 48 hours, I can transport something to any place in the world. This means that suddenly we can achieve a totally different quality of service. I do not have to worry so much about my own foresight; I must have an information system network that I can use to set this process of transportation into movement immediately.

SCHEER There is, however, a bottleneck because I cannot transport materials at the same speed that I can transport information. In my opinion, that will contribute to an enormous reevaluation of the entire logistics in the near term. You also see how suddenly new types of businesses develop. We are lagging behind the international competition here in Germany with our logistics businesses because we are not achieving the size of the Americans with businesses like FedEx. The performance between industry and such logistics partners is shifting so that totally new structures are appearing in this environment.

PLATTNER The logistics partners are taking on more work and also preparing a part of the commercial process in a way that all I need to do is accept delivery. The transport enterprise deals with the complete process of transport, insurance, and customs. This does not mean, however, that I do not have to enter the results in my enterprise business system. It will be simpler and more comfortable, but I must still have an enterprise business system.

The role of the logistics partner

You can also turn the question around the other way: Does the enterprise business system then have less importance compared to all these systems? You must put the question in terms of statistics. There is a multitude of service systems with a high rate of growth on the Internet. Each business, however, has only its own business system.

SCHEER It is, however, a question of how broadly you define this when the boundaries are expanding, and this enterprise system also encompasses those services it can get from others.

The virtual nature of the enterprise system

PLATTNER The marketplace creates connections between enterprises. With the help of the workplace that creates the integration for the user, we direct the view of the employee toward the total process. This total process includes the transportation business, the service businesses, the Internet broker, and so on.

SCHEER What, then, is your opinion about how the enterprises will develop? There are two different ideas. The first idea is that the business of the future will be a small one that makes use of a large network and is very fast, can change partners very rapidly, and thinks more in terms of projects. That is one side. On the other side, every day you read in the newspapers that enterprises are getting bigger and bigger and one merger follows another. This means there is a contradiction between what you think about how the enterprises should look in the future and the real developments. What effect do these tendencies have on your system concept?

A global nature is determined by size

PLATTNER Well, I believe that the difference is this: If an enterprise will really be active on a global basis and actually support the global markets, it just has to be big. A small global enterprise is a contradiction in itself.

SCHEER The actual resources that will give an enterprise strength in the future will be access to the market, sales, access to knowledge, and engineering.

PLATTNER Just as the process chains now stretch out beyond the enterprise, they also stretch out over geographic zones. Through the union in Europe, we have created a larger market; that is, the process chains will run beyond our historical borders. Therefore, an enterprise must have at least a Europe-wide basis if it wants to support these process chains. If I also want to expand this to the world, then I have to be active worldwide. I must have worldwide relationships, and I must have a worldwide presence, and this means the enterprise will have to be big. Sure, there can be an economically interesting niche for a very local provider. But this rests on things that can be ordered worldwide over the Internet and can be delivered by air within 48 hours by UPS, FedEx, DHL, or Deutsche Post.

It is much the same with consulting firms. We have on one side the small society, a few partners, perhaps of very high quality, very exclusive, with their headquarters in Frankfurt. In contrast, we have the global companies—Andersen Consulting, Arthur Andersen,

McKinsey, PriceWaterhouseCoopers. We have both, the globally operating companies, very large and present everywhere, and the specialists, small companies, limited to a few subjects and to a certain market.

SCHEER Clearly, but the big enterprises are the only important ones. Or you can scale down to a very small niche where you take advantage of special know-how or a good location. Then, however, you are limited right from the start in your growth.

PLATTNER The mid-sized businesses have a tendency to be swallowed up. At least it is that way with software publishers. This is a general tendency among service provider companies, and I believe that this idea of being quick and nimble is only for a start-up phase when the intended purpose of the enterprise is being explored and sought. After that the growth laws apply very soon, and they shift noticeably in the direction of globalization.

The mid-sized service providers will be swallowed up

SCHEER Now people speak of B-to-B, business-to-business, and B-to-C, business-to-consumer, as if they were two different worlds. We have spoken only about B-to-B so far. Is the B-to-C world totally different then, or are certain structures not necessary? For example, trust management: When you order something, you are sure the goods will come; when you have paid beforehand, you are sure the goods will come afterwards; or when someone gets the goods, you are sure they will pay for them afterwards. That means the rapid processes are perhaps not so well documented in the virtual world as previously, where you knew your suppliers very well, where you already had your quality index and your price index, and knew whether he was trustworthy. Everything is moving faster and you look for things by price, so you also have to trust the supplier that he will perform his job in the proper manner. Will there suddenly be a need for services that also have to be included in such a marketplace, but that go beyond the purely technical integration?

Business-to-consumer

PLATTNER Everywhere we use credit cards today, the payment takes place after the service is performed, after we have eaten or after we have spent the night in a hotel. We hand over our credit card beforehand, but we sign the slip only afterwards. If I do not sign the slip, I get the bill anyway. There is really only a marginal difference, but the service is used when I order something, I define the entire process, I give someone my credit card number, but it is actually debited when the delivery or the service takes place.

Who wins in the Internet game?

SCHEER What I wanted to discuss is the fact that just such an enterprise as SAP, which has established itself and is not a start-up, can provide its partners in such new business processes with an additional benefit through its size and its responsible nature. The businesses trust that the processes will function technically, but they also trust that the processes will be taken care of from the commercial standpoint afterwards, and this can be something that SAP brings with it.

PLATTNER In relation to our two projects, marketplace and workplace, it is naturally a benefit that SAP has been there over a number of years and that SAP has just been ranked as an "AA enterprise" in relation to its creditworthiness—the best enterprise in Germany, by the way. It also plays a role here that we have customer relations with more than 20,000 companies; that has value in and of itself. The Internet world, in any case, as perhaps a quasi-revolutionary movement, has a certain arrogance in its opinion that the old or established enterprises would not have anything to do with it.

I keep reading again and again that we are not being given credit for this. Recently someone wrote that SAP had received the kiss of death, and he could not see how we could recover from it. Someone puts that on the table, and what do I conclude from it? There is a subliminal arrogance that such an established enterprise cannot do something like this. And there is also a bit of truth in it. A European enterprise will have difficulties in this. I will not express it in any harsher terms.

The world that is now growing on the Internet is seeing only these small services—www.e-bay.com, www.price-line.com, or www.amazon.com—and does not see the overarching whole, that these are only small, rapid service providers. When you take into account the entire services an enterprise needs, or if you look into their share in the services as a sum of all the enterprises—that is, the services provided throughout the world—then you can see that they are playing only a very small part. Every airline is more important—not worth as much on the market, but more important.

I think the time for larger enterprises that can offer long-term stability is just now coming. And people are already writing about things in this direction and say, "Just wait, this Internet game has not been going on for long and is just now starting."

SCHEER We have spoken in detail about this cultural revolution at SAP from R/2 to R/3. Would you compare the current developments with this, or is it even more dramatic?

The new challenge: to change the processes

PLATTNER Clearly more dramatic. As you said previously, we are now changing the processes. We are thinking differently and we have other possibilities, both organizational and in business administration. What is happening is much more in business administration, and these are not well-trodden paths, but new territory. Actually, most of the time we have technically improved on the well-trodden paths. The further into the back office we go, the more well-traveled the paths are. Now, in contrast, we have to make new processes with some technology. It is not a matter of getting there technically 100 percent and once and for all. The technology is constantly changing.

We are making totally new processes and that is the difference. We make totally different demands on the

The SAP main building (DSC) on Neurott Street.

employees, in part very dramatic ones. We ask for imagination, and then they have to transform it. We have positioned ourselves as I just described it. On one hand, we want to show imagination, and on the other hand, we want to do this in a multifaceted way—both, and that is a difficult task. And I believe it is a task that only such an enterprise as SAP could perform.

Scheer Have you thought about spinning this entire area off into something entirely new? That you would say, let's start a new enterprise with just young people, they should do it for the first time, and then we sell the old system as a cash cow for as long as we can.

Plattner This would hurt the good name of SAP. I think it would be bad for SAP, and I have voted against us doing such a thing.

Scheer So it was considered?

Plattner Yes, of necessity. It was said that we should create a new company and new share options and so on. Let the old SAP shareholders see how they manage. Well, they would have been the indirect owners of this company.

SCHEER This means that you went the difficult way of bringing the cultural revolution into your home yourself.

PLATTNER I believe that the company must truly experience mySAP.com, get a feel for it, and then develop the enthusiasm for it. It is not a matter of doing the known thing better in a technical way, as we did in recent years in improving things with R/3, which we knew well. Indeed, new production procedures enter into it, other philosophies of business, like virtual businesses. But we have essentially fought for the technical execution to develop high volume, fine-tune the processes, and improve the user interface.

As in the beginning

The invention of new processes is something different. It is somewhat like a return to the beginning years of SAP. Because of this, I also feel great here. At that time, we went into the business and set up new things, for example, moving part of the accounting to purchasing. We then did the auditing there. At the time, it was natural for us. For most of the accounting people, it was a revolution.

SCHEER Yes, it was, in fact. You carried out a business administration revolution.

PLATTNER We just brought two things together, the purchasing that carried out the operation itself and had all the data and the accounting that has the regulations and properly processes the procedure for later inspection. And we brought the two of them together. Where did they come together? Well, where the data comes in, at billing. Now, however, entire applications are being outsourced, whether it is transportation or services, providing services. If someone does the entire purchasing for me, then the interface has to have a new concept. How does the data come into the enterprise then?

Requirements for an outsourcing solution

Let's take a company like SAP. We outsource everything that SAP purchases to a purchasing professional, and he says he will get a 10 percent reduction in costs each

Hasso Plattner speaks at the general meeting of SAP AG in Mannheim, 1997.

year and guarantees it. That sounds good. What does he need then? He needs an organizational structure in his system that is just as complicated as SAP is. He must know us. He must know every delivery point, he must know that we are in Hamburg, he must know that Hamburg is in Germany because he must send the bill to SAP AG in Germany. In France, he has to send it to another company. He really must know the entire organizational structure of our company and reflect it in his information system. Everyone who is now offering an outsourcing service underrates this point. We have had a little experience with using the same outsourcer in Germany and in America. Today he cannot use the same system.

Business process outsourcing

I believe in this outsourcing, in this specialization on process outsourcing. But this also means that the processing outsourcing systems must have the same complexity and configuration potential as, for example, our enterprise systems now have, because they are enterprise systems. Grainger, for example, does this with jobs. They built a multi-job system for SAP and now service the customers as jobs within it. Then there is a job accounting, and it goes to the enterprise for which they operate the process outsourcing system. We must build the appropriate interfaces for the customers' systems. That is a development in which we see the processes differently. The world will not become much simpler through this, however. The complexity of an enterprise—that is, the geographic complexity, the product complexity, the legal complexity that goes along with the geographic diversity, the language complexity—will continue to exist. At this time, this is totally underrated. But perhaps this is good. You need euphoria at first and then you see that you must still do a lot of work on the details.

Scheer May I return to the point of B-to-B or B-to-C? Do you see a big difference there for SAP? Because it is now going into retail and such things, it suddenly also has consumers to serve in a certain way as customers from the system standpoint. This brings with it some very different things, the billing procedures will be different, and so on.

Plattner So far, we have not been that successful with our B-to-C initiative. We set up shops ourselves and got customers right away, at the start in 1996, and then we lost momentum. Mainly because others concentrated on it. We did it nicely, rapidly; we did crazy things, confused things on the Internet. In 1997 we considered how we could make the shop as maintenance friendly as possible. That was not the subject. And that is an interesting development.

Involvement in the B-to-C area

It was much more important to be able to make a shop rapidly, the variations and particular arrangement of a company, and to make the brand name of a company visible in the shop than it was to create the connection to the logistics chain. Then we developed the alternative "Pandesic," a complete solution that runs very successfully at the companies. The number of Pandesic customers is steadily rising. Eventually, we will see results, and now there are a couple of very good brand names on it. We are going full steam ahead with it and again operating the B-to-C side.

A prerequisite is, and this was a problem for us, that it be project oriented. It is a project business. We are a long ways from someone being able to buy a shop off the rack, and we might never get to that point. There are prefabricated construction elements, but then they must be assembled in an individual way—as in building construction. A lot is planned beforehand and prefabricated, but do you really want a prefabricated house? A business who can afford it will not want that. It will want its own Internet home, its own Internet shop. And all the people involved in this will show up with their brand-new ideas. You will have to include whatever was invented just yesterday, and this can happen only on a project basis.

We have now reorganized ourselves in order to be able to implement this. The B-to-B and B-to-C lines run together in a development group, and this essentially means that we must build the software, the framework for the software, in a way that allows us to integrate the greatest number of software components very easily, technically very easily.

Thoughts on service on the Internet

If I want to sell shoes over the Internet, I need at least high resolution, and I probably also need 3D viewing capability so that I can look at them from all sides. I need what television can do. It presents an image to me. If you watch the television sales shows in which jewelry and such things are sold, someone talks and talks and then the product is turned and displayed so that you have a three-dimensional feel for the item. Then you make the buy or do not buy decision. It is therefore necessary to build in the best or most cost-effective 3D presentation software if I want to sell goods like this.

For another type of merchandise, it is perhaps important that I offer assembly service over the Internet.
Suppose I buy, for example, some furniture; this is our
demonstration model on which we are currently working. I buy some furniture that has to be assembled at
home. If I cannot assemble it, I can access the service
where I just press a button on the Internet and I get
right to the call center where someone shows me
how to assemble it. He does not refer me to the
multi-language assembly instructions that I do not
understand.

You need such a service. On the sales side, you must
be very strongly oriented to the customer. You must be
able to offer the customer something special, or else
the store is a better solution and the Internet is just a
short-lived fad.

SCHEER What I have found very important is this extension
that, despite the overall chaos in the last 20 years, has
been a tremendous stability in the development. This is
the view of business processes where earlier you
looked only at functions. We have analyzed the
processes and only now noticed that part of the financial accounting does not belong at all in the function,
but rather must be included in the process differently.
This was the first big development orientation, the integration of processes.

Continuity of the thought process

The extension consists of going out beyond the boundaries of the enterprise, and there you only do the same
thing that you were doing before. You must think about
what belongs where; what do I receive from another
partner, and where do I have the interfaces? From
there, despite the hectic nature, you do not have many
breaks, but you are simply thinking in total procedures:
Who is involved in this, who has what conditions, and
how am I trying to make these processes as slimmed
down as possible?

PLATTNER The shift is more from material and personnel control to services controlling. Services controlling is something new, but we all know that it is not simple.

SCHEER Many new concepts, for example, the responsibility for the order procedure, naturally also come along with individual items. Look at modern automobile production: it is paid for only upon demand. When the part is put into a car, the parts list is sent back, and only then does the supplier receive his money. But before the part is installed in its final place, the supplier is still the owner and still responsible for the logistics. Many things are shifting already.

PLATTNER No matter how great a revolution this is, it is still a continuation of our business activities, and it is also the application of the digital technology in support of our business activities.

Software demonstration on the Internet But I want to point out something else that brings change and has already brought it about. Software is always something mystifying. You cannot get hold of it properly; it is depicted as something other than what it is; it is really not properly shown because it is something boring and too expensive for most of the participants. Therefore, software is spoken of on an abstract level. When you see the product at some time, there is more or less a great disappointment that the introduction of a software product is such a demanding task and that perhaps not everything presented actually works. There is really no way to check out software before you buy it.

What the Internet companies have done on the small scale, we now want to do on a large scale. We want to make our industry-specific demonstration systems available free on the Internet. Not only partners and customers, but also those who are not customers—competitors—can log on and take a look at our systems. The automobile manufacturers can buy a competitor's model, take it apart, see how it is built, and draw their own conclusions from it. Every consumer buys a car only when he has touched, stroked, and sat in the car beforehand. A test drive is a totally natural thing. And really everything is like this, where you can take a look and try it out before buying it, except for services, of course, because they come later.

Software is a kind of product. I can take a look at it beforehand. And we believe that providing such systems will force our competitors to do the same thing, and seeing who has what to offer, you can make a comparison.

For two years there has been a college in Germany that does software comparisons. We can put our installations there in the latest condition and we can repair the errors; we are allowed to do that. All of the studies and all of the comparisons are done by the college. The results are published within the framework of graduate work or doctoral work. In the evaluations, SAP always comes out very well and, indeed, significantly better than when we win at a sales exhibition. That is, there is always somewhat of a gap between the presentation of a product and talking about it, as opposed to when you actually get hold of it. You can talk about a product being great, but when someone gets hold of it, other qualities come out.

Who would have thought that the R/3 system 4.0B is far and away the best ergonomically in comparison with PeopleSoft, Oracle, and Baan? I would have had my doubts about it because we saw the pretty pictures that PeopleSoft and the others have. When measured in terms of a certain number of transactions with a certain number of users, a somewhat different picture develops.

With the Internet, it is possible for software to be comparable so that people who are in England, America, and Germany can simultaneously work with the information on a demo system that otherwise is not available in the sales process because the system is not yet

Globally test and compare software

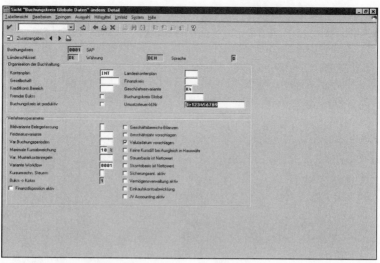

User screens for R/3 release 4.0B.

ready. Otherwise, you can only talk about it. You give the English a demo, the Americans a demo, and the Germans a demo, and it turns out when they all get together that they all saw something different, and all understood something different because it was only a presentation. They never had the time to work with the system.

We still do not know what kind of computer performance it provides and perhaps we will have to lease it out over the Internet so that we can recover our costs, but the idea itself that a system is available worldwide, that was given to us by the Internet.

Future requirements of the software business

SCHEER Look at what the Internet brings: an insane general transparency, collaboration, but also negative things. I believe that there will be problems with copyright. You must also consider how to discuss such things. The copyright is, I believe, at most 200 years old. If you look at a manuscript from the Middle Ages, you do not find any author's name there. Some monk drew it up, and it never crossed his mind to put his name on it. That only started later with printed material. Goethe negotiated with his publisher at that time. Before that, there was no copyright. It might disappear again through copying. You might be able to make money only through different versions that come out rapidly one after the other.

PLATTNER Or through integration.

SCHEER Yes, the broker who brings something together, he will still earn something.

PLATTNER Some people radically say that software is really for free and only the services cost, but I would consider that going too far. I would rather say that the software is free, but when you turn it on and use it, then it costs something. In any case, we are moving toward the idea that we want to lower the threshold for acquiring software. We had a long discussion at SAP, where my colleague at the time, Paul Wahl, was vehemently against it.

Henning Kagermann, member of the board since 1991 and board spokesman, along with Hasso Plattner, since 1999.

We want to make the entrance threshold for acquiring software—and here Henning Kagermann and I are in absolute agreement—as low as it can be. The company who wants to install SAP software extensively always makes a big commitment because it is determined by the fact that the project is starting now, that internal momentum will be created, and that he wants to get the maximum discount.

The ambivalence of technical updating

SCHEER We cannot discuss the business effects of the Internet in detail here, but in terms of how it affects each of us, certainly one of the aspects is the enormous transparency. There is a transparency between enterprises, but it also affects the private area. It is going so far that some say there is a threat of a person losing his privacy because he can constantly be located through GPS (Global Positioning System), and so on.

PLATTNER Yes, right, but only when I have a GPS with me.

SCHEER But you can also do it over a cell phone. Obviously people are not all that worked up about this. Some people even make money by installing a camera in their bathrooms so you can watch them wash up in the morning.

PLATTNER These are peculiarities, and I don't know whether that is normal.

SCHEER Certainly not, but perhaps we have also raised issues that people consider dangerous.

PLATTNER There is a change, I believe, in what we perceive as normal and what we perceive as a threat. I have said many times that the mail I constantly receive is a larger threat. All kinds of people get my address somewhere and have a couple of my attributes. They send me mail based on these attributes. It has "personal" written on it, I must open the letter, and so on. It would be a lot easier to get this as email. Then I could take care of it immediately; I would not have to open it and do all the other things that go along with it. And you could probably take defensive measures through software. If I get it in digital form, I can check the contents against keywords and, when necessary, place the email so far back in my priority ranking that I never get around to looking at it.

What burdens me is this mail I receive, and I see that the Internet will probably improve the situation and not make it worse. It is the same with many things. When the telephone arrived, you could constantly call someone. So the telephone also has a negative effect. And the cell phone: Wherever you go, they disturb you. Sooner or later, mobile telephones will be forbidden in restaurants just as smoking cigarettes is.

SCHEER Already such signs forbid not only smoking cigarettes, but also using cell phones.

PLATTNER Well, wonderful. I have not seen them yet, but that is exactly what has to happen. For example, on the golf course. Soon it will be common etiquette that you do not take your cell phone on the golf course.

We are changing our rules and standards. We have seen lengthy discussion about the misuse of the Internet and the criminal actions on the Internet. There naturally is that potential, because it is far easier to break in on the Internet than to break through glass. It is a different quality. With glass, I smash it, and on the Internet, I hack in. But what is the negative side for the ones breaking in, the Internet criminals? Everything is recorded and traceable. The last case in which people used the Internet for criminal purposes was cleared up in detail within a week. Digital systems are also transparent.

Transparency on the Internet

SCHEER This also means, however, that you lose privacy when such things can be traced.

PLATTNER Yes, Mr. Clinton fell victim to this. His telephone calls were traceable in detail.

A prognosis **SCHEER** If you dare offer a prognosis—and you also have to make such decisions, for Germany, Europe, the US, and Asia—how would you see the penetration of this thinking that you previously laid out?

PLATTNER Well, it is obvious that America is clearly out in front at this time.

SCHEER Despite this, can someone also be successful working from Germany?

PLATTNER First of all, I believe that this is taking place worldwide. In South Africa, a person does his shopping over the Internet the same as elsewhere in the world. There is a time lag involved, but it is not the case that such shopping does not happen in one country but is total in another country. It is only a question of the speed. Sweden and the Nordic countries will adapt to this faster than others. Everywhere a technology already is in place, or where a high level of affinity for technology exists, it will happen faster.

The newspaper just reported that the new science minister or economics minister in South Africa wants to make a large investment in Internet technology so that access is available just about everywhere and purchasing can happen over the Internet. This means in every village, even those with no connections for electricity, I will soon be able to communicate worldwide over the Internet by satellite. This happens faster than laying copper or fiber optic lines.

I believe that this networking information between consumers and suppliers, just as between companies, is a movement that cannot be stopped.

Chapter 6

Integration and Diversity

Outlook by Hasso Plattner

I believe it is still not clear to many people where the true potential lies when you can control and operate applications of various kinds with point and click.

The last of the conversations documented in this book took place six months ago and, in relation to current developments, that is half an eternity in an Internet generation. I therefore want to take the comments on SAP's newest Internet initiative further with some remarks on the opportunities and risks of mySAP.com from today's viewpoint. With this new product, but not for the last time, SAP has tackled the very difficult task of reinventing itself. It's no easy undertaking, but so far it's a successful one, partly because the employees of SAP AG throughout the world have joined in with their efforts and persisted in an admirable way. Now, at the beginning of the year 2000, I can say, "The basic concept of mySAP.com is correct and will be accepted by the market, that is, by both existing and new SAP customers."

There is a clear tendency in enterprises to give the greatest possible number of employees access to information available in digital form and steadily growing. People also increasingly recognize that enterprises who do not include their employees in these capabilities are hardly competitive any more. Therefore the mySAP.com workplace has enormous importance.

The portal strategy: mySAP.com workplace

The mySAP.com workplace is a portal through which employees gain access to the applications of the enterprise. They can, however, also use it to access applications outside the enterprise, such as those provided on the Internet. These outside applications might be offers from companies or groups of companies providing their services through their Internet portal; they can also be services from Application Service Providers (ASP) that provide entire applications on the Web and thus simultaneously serve multiple users, that is, multiple companies.

It is proving to be the right strategy that we have settled on this portal technology. As mentioned in previous chapters, in the last few years we have been strongly oriented in our work on user interfaces; the keyword is EnjoySAP. With its improvements, we have not only made things simpler for the user, but have also made it suitable for the Internet. And now that is paying off.

We can, at this time, make a new offer. The users will no longer have to retrieve the individual transactions and reports that are somewhere in the system because SAP can combine it all in a package for the individual groups of users. We call this concept *roles*. In the given role, we bring everything together that is relevant to a certain group of users. When the individual user turns on his PC, he immediately finds on his screen the workplace that he needs to perform his daily tasks. When externally stored programs or applications also belong there, they can also appear on the screen of the workplace. This continuously expandable package contains both the applications for working within the operations and the applications that are important for interactions between enterprises. We can also arrange for general information services and other services, for example, to appear on the workplace.

The marketplace strategy: mySAP.com marketplace
The second essential component of mySAP.com is the marketplace. This relates to applications that serve the communications and development of business between enterprises. The information exchange and

the interaction of enterprises no longer have the nature of a passive transmission of information; active systems will facilitate business partnerships and also implement them. It might be a matter of the most varied types of services, such as transportation, consulting, or digital services. With priceline.com, for example, you can find the cheapest ticket for a flight from Frankfurt to New York; through options offers, you can make contact with all the suppliers of a certain product, and so on. There are almost no limits to the imagination here.

Today we are continually working with better software that makes a higher degree of business administration cooperation possible. The next step will be to produce this cooperation in the earliest phase of product definition between the enterprise that designs with the product and wants to build it and the enterprises that are supposed to help it at the engineering level. This perspective is important for almost all production enterprises, because the degree of cooperation there is still relatively low. The large auto manufacturing companies, for example, have pursued collaborative design internally for years. I am thinking here of Ford. Some time back, a very good marketing initiative showed that Ford was developing things 24 hours a day and exchanging the development documents electronically in doing so.

This will take place in the future not only within a company, but collaborative business will determine the future as a market principle and many enterprises will invent new services; we are experiencing such approaches already. It is henceforth technically possible to connect two or more companies; the high rates of data transmission are available, and the software provides capabilities that were not imagined 20, 10, or even 2 years ago.

In this respect, marketplaces in the future will take on a very decisive importance. Companies will use their influence and their significance in the market to supply such marketplaces with content. They will also attempt to influence these marketplaces in an essential manner, not the least because this promises to become a profitable business. In any case, there will be a whole list of company-specific marketplaces on the Internet. Big enterprises have already begun setting up such marketplaces, and the suppliers of these enterprises will be invited to participate. It will also be an advantage for smaller businesses as well, because a digital connection of this type that will be maintained permanently is naturally different from communications by telephone, fax, or even letter. The exchange of digital data over EDI (Electronic Data Interchange) also cannot compare to such actual transactional connections. In my opinion, the marketplace technology that we have available today, which allows us to set up communications between enterprises that can be operated either by people or automatically by programs, is of a new quality.

Besides the enterprise marketplaces, however, there will also be marketplaces initiated by associations, and there will naturally be marketplaces run by states. I already see such a development in Germany with its Bundesländern. In brief, wherever there is a strong community with the corresponding infrastructure and a "customer territory"—that is, a political institution, an association, an enterprise of appropriate importance—there is the nucleus for an electronic marketplace already at hand. Because applications software and the corresponding technologies are important in this realm, it is also of considerable importance for SAP—but not only because a new field of activity is developing here and thereby creating further opportunities for SAP to strengthen existing business relationships and to build up new ones. These new applications reach much deeper into the enterprise. They will in part even replace applications that today exist within an enterprise.

Example: the change in the purchasing systems

Purchasing systems are an example. For more than 25 years, purchasing systems have been a component part of the applications systems in an enterprise. All purchasing systems rest upon the idea that they absorb a part of the market knowledge and store it in catalogs within the enterprise. Finally, people who want to buy access these catalogs. But, and this is a decisive disadvantage, the enterprises must constantly maintain these catalogs. Each enterprise maintains its own supplier catalog for itself, and within the supplier catalog the product data must be maintained in turn.

An obviously more efficient possibility would be that several enterprises divide the cost of this maintenance. Doing this would bring a saving in costs on one hand and an increase in quality on the other hand because more information would come together. In this case, the catalogs would be kept outside the data processing of any individual enterprise. That is, they must be "hosted" in one place and kept there, which is not dissimilar to a marketplace. And exactly this is already happening; some catalog producers build, maintain, and then offer to multiple companies their complete catalog for certain electronic components or a catalog for chemical products.

Today, however, it is also technically possible to access directly the catalog of products offered by an individual enterprise. Every company will sooner or later have to put its product catalog on the Internet. When you can access this catalog directly, you no longer need to maintain it in the enterprise nor keep it maintained for a group of enterprises. And when the various catalogs of the different companies are moreover so compatible that you can interpret them electronically, then they no longer have to be brought together, but rather can be automatically united as if they were a network of catalogs. For me, it seems to be a generic and almost natural development from the catalogs made by the enterprise itself through the externally maintained and prepared catalog on to the network of catalogs in which the provider maintains the catalog. The possibilities lie in providing applications that can interpret the catalogs.

Networks of catalogs

In many cases, purchasing also includes the need to regulate the conditions between the selling and the buying business. The selling company has its idea of the conditions that it offers its customers. This normally has the consequence that a sales system with appropriate components contains the stated conditions for the various customer categories. In addition, within the customer categories are still more differences according to the customer sales, the importance, or the other individual product groups. Each purchasing company, on the other hand, also has its idea of how it will do its buying, and depending on its importance and its commercial relationships with the selling company, it naturally tries to impose its conditions. The electronic commerce content will thus be based in significant part on the specific conditions.

A system in the middle would be necessary. Even when you start with the idea that such systems are viable in the marketplaces, they must be in a position to provide special conditions, even when they are generic systems for everyone. And that is difficult. I therefore believe that a considerable part of the software that will remain in the enterprises will no longer serve to maintain the totality of the information, that is, the catalog, but rather only the conditions specific to the company. The catalog itself is, in contrast, common goods.

Integration of the marketplace and the enterprise's own business systems

This tendency is currently unmistakable and has rapidly accelerated over the past six months. SAP will make a significant contribution here. The development of the marketplace systems has become the highest priority for us. What is significant for us at SAP, in addition to the development of these new systems, is the fact that we have a special talent. We can connect these new systems with the systems that still have to run in the enterprises, and we will run in them in a way that the transition is seamless for the user. In the future, the user will no longer know just where his software is running.

Let us imagine that SAP users in the next year use their systems in the same way that they would select various services on the Internet through AOL. They surf their way to the various Internet offers and applications systems over a unified navigation system defined and maintained by AOL. They will no longer note whether they are right at the product information data bank in the enterprise, at a data bank with marketing information that a market research business has made available, or on the catalog described earlier. This way of working over various systems is something new.

We have probably believed for too long that we must pack everything into the development of our applications systems. Even small expansions had to be in line with larger ones whose implementation was absolutely essential.

The Internet has taught us another viewpoint: The user has again become the owner of the program!

The user in the sense that he is again the determining factor, and this change is now quite clear. We no longer must provide a technically unified and integrated system that is installed and maintained as a unit; we can provide several systems, as long as we do not burden the user in doing so. That sole criterion is important. If the user does feel burdened—either through different navigation mechanisms or the differing presentations of the various systems so that various interfaces cause confusion—then the demand for technical integration will come at once. Here at SAP, however, we have shown with mySAP.com that we can implement unified navigation and presentation with the help of portal technology, which is an essential component of our concept.

The portal technology is also a great liberation for SAP as a developmental publisher. It specifically makes parallel development easier. We can develop more things faster and provide a looser integration on

The primacy of functional integration

the programming side. By looser integration, we do not mean that the data will no longer be exchanged between the systems, but that the exchange between the systems that are physically independent of each other is accomplished by self-describing documents like XML, in the same way it is performed with the physical integration of the systems. A prerequisite is, however, that the functional integration is kept intact for the user when doing this.

Looking into the future, this means that I have a very positive feeling about SAP and the development of the enterprise. It looks like the mySAP.com workplace is already being accepted. The total concept of looking at the world from the point of view of the user has proven to be the right one in any case, beginning with the EnjoySAP initiative and moving to the SAP workplace now available. Naturally, this process is not yet concluded. Skeptics still ask themselves, and others, whether SAP will succeed in implementing this concept and maintaining its position against competition, especially when you see how high the newest Internet enterprises are now valued.

An interesting aspect of this lies in the question, "Are only the small enterprises nimble enough to be able to implement new ideas, or are the mega-mergers that we have lately experienced the only ones with the necessary critical mass to perform the tasks of the future?" I am convinced that as soon as the tendencies have visibly solidified, and as soon as it is clear which way the path goes, the bigger enterprises have at least the same chances long-term, perhaps even better. In any case, it is a matter of a clear increase in the quality of our digital systems, taken all together.

To recognize trends and act cooperatively

I consider it first of all important that big enterprises such as SAP recognize the trends in a timely manner. Because as long as you have not recognized the new trends, you cannot properly utilize the "muscle" of the big company. Secondly, you must recognize that there will not be any stable conditions, particularly in a dynamic market of this type. There will always be something new arriving; there will always be something coming along that overtakes and improves on the principles that have just been established. This means that an enterprise, if it wants to survive, must possess one thing above all, an enormous openness to be able to work cooperatively with others.

At SAP, we have first of all avoided the first of these dangers, that of overlooking the trends. I believe that we have a clear picture of what the future will look like in the upcoming three years. The second danger of not being open enough to work with others is less a technological, than a mental problem, one of the company's culture.

This is especially true because every potential partner has the tendency to expand as rapidly as possible, particularly in our business world that is determined by risk capital and stock market capital, where even the small enterprises grow rapidly and the danger of overlap is greater. This makes partnerships more difficult. But nevertheless, these two aspects—to recognize which way things are going and put one's energy into that area and to be open to partnerships—are the necessary prerequisites for being able to provide this integration that reaches beyond company boundaries and applications.

I believe it is still not clear to many people where the true potential lies when you can control and operate applications of various kinds with point and click. Bill Gates, until recently chairman of the board and now chief of the supervisory board of Microsoft, had carried out a campaign for years for point and click and drag and drop and thus revolutionized office applications. Now it is going far beyond these office applications, just as it is going far beyond the transactional business applications of SAP. Now you can build applications with a totally different intelligence. One example that

The multimedia nature and information diversity

we are currently showing in our Customer Relationship Management prototype is the connection of a so-called GIS system (Graphical Information System) with a data warehouse with the aid of transactional systems. In the next step, we will also be able to connect information that is available on the Internet. With this new type of business intelligence solution, I can get a picture at almost the speed of thought of what the relationship looks like in a certain region of the earth between the market potential and the market penetration. More-over, I can rapidly acquire information on the products that are being sold in this region. I can go into the structure with one click and find out who is taking on what jobs in this region. I can determine at a glance whether we are lagging behind, stagnating, or facing an exponential growth ahead of us, and from this I can immediately take actions—such as change something in the management of the region or set marketing actions in progress. This is truly new, that I can see these facts. For as long as I have been doing data processing, I have felt the deficiency in the fact that we do not understand the information on a spreadsheet as directly as we do the spoken word or visual informa-tion. The visual presentation of an empty office, for example, shows me immediately that something is not right with the business.

Breaking out of the abstract data world

Over the past 25 years, we have dealt with a very abstract world in data processing. We have built a nar-row digital reflection of reality. With the possibilities of the Internet, we are beginning to break out of this abstract world. To stick with the example of a GIS sys-tem: A very different quality of information is presented when I can use such a system and display directly on a map how the market potential and the sales volumes stand in relation to each other.

Even when I was in school, it fascinated me that you can access information from totally different sources.

On the one hand, you can look at the statistics for something like where on the earth oil is to be found. Then you find out that Saudi Arabia is at the top and that there is also oil in Nigeria. This is only somehow interesting. If you look at the same information on a map, however, it opens up additional aspects. You begin to connect information of different kinds with each other. And this is something totally different from reading a spreadsheet, even when it is so nicely sorted by percentages.

With the Internet, we are now for the first time truly in a position of being able to provide two- or even three-dimensional information in parallel with our coded world of data processing. Still, test-driving a car or listening to a stereo set before buying are naturally not made redundant by this. This is more a matter of things that I, as an individual, cannot actually experience. For example, it would be a real experience for me if I could drive along with Mika Haekkinen or Michael Schumacher on various racetracks of the world via the Internet. We can already have that experience on the television, and it is sharply different from the actual day-to-day driving of a car. The capabilities of the Internet place us collectively in the position of being able to experience things that we otherwise could not really experience. A noteworthy visual transformation here is, in my opinion, the Intel advertising of some years ago, which worked so well with "Intel inside." To move around by helicopter "in" a chip, that is, to get a tour of this chip at the micrometer scale or even smaller dimensions—that can happen only in this way and manner. The senses are drawn into our "real" experience. These advertising spots ran both on the television and in movie theaters, but in principle it is also conceivable for procedures on the Internet. There will be, in my opinion, a different quality that you can additionally provide in the business processes. I see an explosive development approaching us in this.

The possibility of multi-dimensional information

Hans-Georg Plaut once said that before you start a pro-ject, you have to visit the enterprises concerned. Those of us who produce software have almost always looked on this type of contact as superfluous. We had an abstract picture of an enterprise, and because the soft-ware is also an abstract depiction, we saw no necessity for dealing with the reality. At the instigation of Hans-Georg Plaut, we finally made a couple of trips out to companies. And we found out that the real impression you get has an immediate influence on the abstract picture. We therefore over the past decades have always put special value on customer contact by our employees, including those in development. This con-nection between the coded and the real world will become increasingly important as the Internet pro-motes these procedures. It will change the world of information processing.

Beginning with EnjoySAP, we have again learned that we must observe people at their work much more. We must work with them and grasp how they work or how they would like to work. We cannot just simply install a system for them and say, "You will have to deal with it!" With mySAP.com, SAP takes this point of view. This point of view alone guarantees that the connection between the real and the abstract worlds can be con-verted into coding.

The Earth seems to be spinning much faster and the worlds coming closer together because of the Internet, not least among other things. What counts is informa-tion, and whoever has information available more rapidly than the others will be among the successful ones. Of course, today many people simply cannot participate in this trend. Our digitized world requires certain talents that not everyone possesses to the same degree. It is obvious that years of training in abstract thought, such as working with computers and software, make it easier to deal with this world. People with higher and longer education have a very clear advantage.

On the other hand, the Internet is geographically independent. This means that there is no longer any advantage to one's location. If the visions become reality and the Internet achieves the importance that libraries and archives—and possibly also television—have today, then it can contribute to a democratization of information.

For example, the availability of universities' content worldwide presents a great opportunity. And when the networks are so fast that we can attend the lectures at the various universities live throughout the entire world, then we are one step further along. It would also be technically conceivable to integrate the Internet and television to create a single information network world-wide that makes all existing information available to all people. This means that in the not too distant future, each person would have available the same potential knowledge. But this also means that we must ensure that the educational standards worldwide have compa-rable quality; in the end, everyone must be able to understand that they can use this potential and know how to use it.

We have to work on this. This is, in my opinion, per-haps the greatest challenge for the future. Humanity must be in the position to define a truly worldwide, fundamental right to education and to guarantee its protection.

The Hasso Plattner Timeline

January 21, 1944	Born in Berlin.
1963–1968	Studied communications engineering (TU Karlsruhe). Diploma awarded in engineering.
1968–1972	Employee at IBM Germany.
April 1, 1972	SAP founded.
1973–1977	Concentrated on further developing financial accounting into a standard package and implementing it for customers.
From 1978	Concentrated on the basic technology of SAP systems. Project director in the development of dialogue control, online documentation, programmable data acquisition interfaces, buffer algorithms, and performance optimization.
1979	Assumed overall responsibility for the technology field. Initiated the SAP thrust into the client/server field.
1987	Directed the fundamental work for new development of SAP systems.
1988	Member of the board (deputy chairman) of SAP AG, software technology: ➤ Applications architecture. ➤ Software quality assurance. ➤ Applications in accounting. ➤ Documentation and translation.

1990	Awarded honorary doctorate from the University of Saarbrücken.
1994	Awarded honorary professor at the University of Saarbrücken.
	Professor for the specialized field of economics.
1996	Broke the record, held for more than 20 years, for the Sydney-Hobart Regatta in his sea-going yacht *Morning Glory*, for which he programmed the steering.
1997	Was presented the Computerworld Smithsonian Award.
	Speaker for the board of SAP AG:
	➤ Development basis, technology, solutions for industry branches.
	➤ Manager of the research and development center in Palo Alto, USA.
1998	Inducted into the German Hall of Fame (*Manager* magazine).
	Endowment of the Hasso Plattner Institute for Software Systems Technology in Potsdam. The Institute is to conduct research in cooperation with the University of Potsdam and provide scientific education for engineers in software systems technology.
	Honorary senator at the University of Saarbrücken.
1999	Responsible for the SAP Internet strategy mySAP.com, including marketing, communications, and openness work.

The SAP Timeline

1972	SAP (System analysis program development) is founded as a partnership in April by former IBM system consultants Dietmar Hopp, Hasso Plattner, Klaus E. Tschira, Hans-Werner Hector, and Claus Wellenreuther. The company is located in Weinheim. The office opens in Mannheim, but all five founders work mainly in the computer centers of their customers. The first job comes from ICI, a man-made fiber plant in Östringen. System R is developed for ICI. The "R" stands for real time. At the end of the first business year, SAP has nine employees, and the turnover is about 620,000 DM.
1976	SAP GmbH Systems, Applications, and Products in data processing is founded as an assistance and sales enterprise. Five years later, the partnership is dissolved and its rights transferred to SAP GmbH.
1977	The company and business headquarters move from Weinheim to Walldorf.
1978	SAP begins a project with John Deere. The first French version of the accounting arrives on the market.
1979	SAP gets the first Siemens large computer of its own with two megabytes of working memory. SAP begins research on the R/2 system.
1980	SAP moves into the first building of its own in Walldorf.

	The SAP co-founder Claus Wellenreuther leaves the enterprise for health reasons.
1981	The completely reworked System R is put on the market as R/2.
	SAP first attends a fair at Systems in Munich.
1982	In SAP's 10th year, the turnover is around 24 million DM. More than 250 enterprises in German-speaking countries are working with SAP software. The number of employees reaches 100.
1984	SAP opens its first foreign branch office in Biel, the SAP (International) AG.
1985	SAP begins developing the new system R/3.
1986	SAP is present at the CeBIT in Hannover for the first time.
	In Austria, the first Land [state] company of SAP is founded.
	The turnover reaches the 100 million mark boundary.
1987	The International Training Center is constructed in Walldorf.
1988	SAP GmbH converts into a joint stock company.
	In October, SAP AG enters the Frankfurt stock exchange.
	SAP North America is founded in Philadelphia.
	Dow Chemicals is the 1,000th customer of SAP.

1989	SAP hosts the first SAPPHIRE user conference in North America.
	Shareholders hold their first general meeting in June in Karlsruhe.
	The R/2 system features a new user-friendly interface.
1990	With the unification of Germany, SAP establishes a presence in the east. Together with Siemens Nixdorf and Robotron, SAP founds the SRS in Dresden. SAP creates a new business office in Berlin.
1991	SAP expands its board to include Prof. Dr. Kagermann in addition to the company founders.
	The client/server technology based R/3 system is presented at the CeBIT.
1992	In SAP's 20th year of operation, the foreign share of the total turnover of 831 million DM reaches the 50 percent level.
	The new Development and Sales Center (DSC) is dedicated.
	SAP software is Y2K compliant.
1993	SAP enters into cooperation with Microsoft. One goal is porting the R/3 system to Windows NT.
	With the construction of a development center in Foster City (USA), SAP establishes a presence in Silicon Valley.
	SAP can supply the Japanese market with an R/3 version in the Kanji alphabet.
	Dr. Peter Zencke becomes a member of the board.

1994	SAP becomes number one among producers of enterprise software.
	SAP delivers the R/3 system for Windows NT.
	SAP wins IBM as a customer for R/3.
1995	SAP shares are included in the DAX.
	Deutsche Telecom and Microsoft decide to use R/3. The order from Deutsche Telecom is the largest in the history of the company.
	Hans-Werner Hector leaves the SAP board and moves to the supervisory board.
1996	SAP together with Microsoft presents its Internet strategy. Internet applications can be connected with the R/3 system over open interfaces. R/3 3.1 is thereby the first Internet-capable business software.
	The AS/400 from IBM is available to customers as a new platform.
	The Union of European Economic Journalists chooses SAP as the Enterprise of the Year.
	Coca-Cola, the largest producer of soft drinks, decides to use R/3.
	New records for attendance are set at the numerous customer exhibitions: At the European SAPPHIRE in Vienna, 4,300 people get information on the products and strategy of SAP, and at the American SAPPHIRE, SAP counts more than 8,000 participants.
	For the third time, SAP is selected as Enterprise of the Year by *Manager* magazine.

	SAP develops ASAP (AcceleratedSAP) as a method for the efficient introduction of R/3.

The SAP board is expanded by three (deputy) members: Claus E. Heinrich, Gerhard Oswald, and Paul Wahl. |
| 1997 | Hasso Plattner is given equal standing along with Dietmar Hopp as spokesman for the SAP board.

SAP celebrates its 25th company anniversary.

SAP and Software AG jointly found the consulting business SAP Systems Integration.

Strategic orientation to specific branches of industry established with the building of 20 Industry Solutions up to this point.

25,000 Motorola users work with the SAP R/3-HR (for personnel matters).

At the end of the year, release 4.0 of the R/3 system is ready. |
| 1998 | A change in leadership: Dietmar Hopp and Klaus Tschira, two of the founders of SAP, move in May from the board to the supervisory board, and Dietmar Hopp takes over the chair. For the second spokesman for the board along with SAP founder Hasso Plattner, the supervisory board selects Henning Kagermann.

With the EnjoySAP initiative, SAP places the user in the center of attention.

The new top value of the SAP stock prices in July is 1,325 DM. |

	On August 3, SAP enters the New York Stock Exchange, the largest stock market in the world.
	SAPPHIRE achieves a new record in visitors in Madrid with 8,000 participants and in Los Angeles with 15,000 participants.
	With the introduction of the New Dimension product family, SAP becomes a multiple-product company.
1999	At the 6th SAPPHIRE users conference in Nizza, Hasso Plattner presents the new products offered for electronic commerce, including for the first time the strategy mySAP.com for developing business over the Internet.
	The mySAP.com Internet Marketplace opens in October.
	In December, SAP announces the establishment of a mySAP.com marketplace related to chemical and pharmaceutical concerns.
	R/3-Release 4.6 contains the newly created Enjoy user interface.
	There are more than 20,000 R/3 installations worldwide.
	R/3 runs on Linux.
2000	SAP starts the decade with a new record high on the stock market of more than 850.

SAP offers application hosting with mySAP.com.

At the heart of the exhibits at CeBIT 2000 is mySAP.com, the new solution concept for the optimal integration of all relevant business process over the Internet.

SAP Turnover Development (in Million DM, Rounded Off)		Number of Employees	
1972	0.6	1972	9
1976	4	1976	25
1982	24	1982	100
1988	245	1988	940
1989	367	1989	1,367
1990	499	1990	2,138
1991	707	1991	2,685
1992	831	1992	3,157
1993	1,101	1993	3,648
1994	1,831	1994	5,229
1995	2,696	1995	6,857
1996	3,722	1996	9,202
1997	6,017	1997	12,856
1998	8,472	1998	19,308
1999	5,110	1999	21,699

A Short SAP Glossary

ABAP Advanced Business Application Programming; the fourth-generation SAP development language. With R/3 release 4.6, the SAP programming language ABAP took a further evolutionary step and became ABAP Objects, a language that incorporates important concepts of object-oriented programming.

AcceleratedSAP A standardized installation method that integrates the newest experiences for the implementation of R/3. With ASAP, you can minimize the time needed for an R/3 installation by up to 50 percent, improve the quality, and, with the efficient use of resources, reduce costs to a minimum.

Advanced Planner and Optimizer A software solution for dynamic supply chain management. Applications for detailed planning, optimization, and termination make possible a precise and global supervision of the logistics chain beyond the bounds of one's own business. APO includes the modules Supply Chain Cockpit, Turnover Planning, Supply Network Planning and Development, Production and Detailed Planning, and Global Availability Verification (see *Available-to-Promise*). Through the combined use of APO and Business Information Warehouse (BW), SAP clients can optimize performance and costs throughout the entire logistics chain.

APO See *Advanced Planner and Optimizer*.

Application hosting A new outsourcing model, according to which businesses no longer operate their hardware and software in-house, but rather outsource it to appropriate service businesses and pay only for the applications that are necessary in each case. The goal is to reduce the costs for both hardware and software, as well as for data processing employees.

ASAP See *AcceleratedSAP*.

Available-to-Promise An application that verifies the availability of materials and components in the distribution centers, production facilities, and warehouses throughout the system, simultaneously, and at various levels. With the Global Availability Verification (Global Available-to-Promise), you can check supply and demand worldwide. See also *Advanced Planner and Optimizer*.

BAPI Business Application Programming Interface. The BAPIs developed by SAP are open and producer-independent interfaces for manipulating business objects in distributed systems. As object methods, BAPIs handle transactions in distant applications and receive any eventual response information in the application itself.

Business framework An integrated, open, and component-based product architecture that includes both the business administration applications components of the R/3 system and the products and technologies of other manufacturers. The SAP business framework makes implementing system upgrades and maintenance easier; provides for close interaction of R/3, older systems, client-specific applications, and the solutions of other manufacturers; and offers a flexible platform for converting changes.

Business Information Warehouse The data warehouse of the new generation for support of strategic and operational business decision-making. It combines the most modern warehousing technology with preconfigured business content and provides a comprehensive overview of the internal, and relevant external, business data. The SAP Business Information Warehouse includes a large selection of predefined report formats that are tailored for the special requirements of certain branches and user groups— production planner, finance controller, personnel director, and so on.

Business Intelligence Solution A comprehensive closed system you can use to make decisions relevant to business. These decisions can be embedded in the operational system and the results can subsequently be monitored. When the information is made available, operational data will be combined with analytic and context-derived knowledge. The basis for the SAP Business Intelligence Solution consists on one hand of the quantitative information from the R/3 system and on the other hand of analytical knowledge that comes from other applications, such as the SAP BW. A third input is context-derived information delivered from the SAP Knowledge Management Applications, such as the SAP Information Database (SAP InfoDB). Together these three pillars support the entire business knowledge base. The "roof of knowledge" on these three pillars consists of the supplemental analytic applications contained in the SAP SEM.

Business scenarios Business processes extending beyond operations with which employees can develop businesses electronically. Business scenarios provide examples of the options of mySAP.com and serve as proposals for the development of our own Internet business processes. Business scenarios not only support users in understanding their roles in the business use of the Internet, but are also useful when entering the Internet business world. See also *mySAP.com.*

Business-to-Business Procurement An innovative comprehensive solution for buying over the Internet. With SAP BBP, every authorized employee has the opportunity to procure goods and services directly from his place of work through a user-friendly, Web-based interface.

BW See *Business Information Warehouse.*

B2B See *Business-to-Business Procurement.*

Collaboration A new level of integrated business development between businesses. The goal of mySAP.com is to promote this new level of cooperation. Procedures that up until now consisted of a number of transactions can be processed in a single step via the Internet and through the marketplace portal of mySAP.com.

Community A group of persons or businesses with common interests who, in order to achieve their goals, actively communicate and work together. Communities who utilize the Web as their communications infrastructure are also called virtual communities. The people and businesses in the SAP environment represent a community or business community. Services and applications support this community as components of the mySAP.com system. In addition, SAP has set up a portal for business communities under www.mysap.com.

CRM See *Customer Relationship Management.*

Customer Relationship Management A product that supports the entire business processes in which clients and external business partners participate. As a comprehensive product for all users with contact with clients, SAP CRM contains solutions for sales (SAP Sales), service (SAP Service), and marketing (SAP Marketing). This involves, on one hand, existing functions of the SAP R/3 system like Customer Service and, on the other hand, new components like Mobile Sales, Mobile Service, and the Customer Interaction Center, as well as Internet Sales. CRM and the Internet scenarios are merging more and more. SAP accommodates this aspect through the integration of SAP CRM in the mySAP.com system. The CRM solutions also make possible interactions between businesses and business partners, such as purchasing, over the Internet.

Employee self-service A concept that makes it possible to actively include the employees in the business processes of personnel administration (HR). Independent of time or location, they can report, enter, or maintain certain data through an easily operated Web browser. Clients and employees gain by having current data, and the personnel department is freed from time-consuming data entry to concentrate on strategic tasks.

EnjoySAP An EnjoySAP initiative whereby SAP is orienting its software towards the needs of the user. The software is thus easier and faster to learn and use and suits the specific work requirements better. As part of this initiative,

SAP has developed a total shell for the creation of a visually attractive, interactive, and personalized user interface related to the user's job duties. The orientation of the software to the personal style of a user's work results in a high level of user satisfaction. The initiative reduces learning time, as well as training costs, and the advantages of standard software for business administration are available to a broad range of users.

Enterprise Resource Planning The market for business administration user software, which SAP helped found. The vision of the 1970s of carrying out business processes in a near real-time dialog with the computer and continually optimizing them has become a reality with SAP's products. With the R/3 system, SAP sets global standards for technology and business administration. R/3 is a family of integrated components (Product, Sales, Controlling, Personnel Administration) that can be installed as a whole or in part. Installed more than 20,000 times, R/3 is used by businesses and organizations of various sizes in a variety of industries. An internationally networked service organization takes care of SAP's clients around the clock and around the world. R/3 is Internet-capable and connects easily with software from third-party providers and the clients themselves.

ERP See *Enterprise Resource Planning.*

ESS See *Employee self-service.*

IDES International Demonstration and Education System; in the R/3 system, a fully developed and integrated model business that serves SAP on an international level as the base system for internal and external training.

Industry solutions Software support tailored for the business processes specific to various industries. SAP has established 13 industry business units (IBUs) since 1997. They bear the product responsibility for one or more of the 20 industry solutions developed to date. These branch solutions were created on the basis of the R/3 system and are constantly refined in close contact with clients and partners. One result of the collaboration are the "blueprints" for the business processes of a branch—the so-called solution maps. They facilitate the systematic conversion of overall information technology solutions from standardized and business-specific components. With this strategic orientation toward branches, SAP is meeting the growing market demand with regard to the individuality and integration capability of software solutions.

Internet Transaction Server The interface between the R/3 system and the Internet. The Internet Transaction Server (ITS) allows users on the Internet and on intranets to communicate directly with the R/3 system so they can start business administration transactions, functional building blocks, and reports as Internet Applications Components (IACs).

ITS See *Internet Transaction Server*.

LES See *Logistics Execution System*.

Logistics Execution System Part of SAP's supply chain management solution, which connects production, procurement, warehousing, distribution, transportation, and sales. SAP LES consists of two applications: Transportation Management and Warehouse Management.

Marketplace In the context of the mySAP.com initiative, a place on the Web in which communities can electronically exchange goods and services. SAP makes one such "marketplace" available under the URL www.mysap.com. See also *mySAP.com*.

mySAP.com A new product of SAP for the best possible utilization of the opportunities the Internet offers. The goal is to strengthen client relationships through increased collaboration by communities, whereby access opportunities are provided around the clock and around the globe. However, mySAP.com should not be confused with the portal www.mysap.com, which provides an entry to the marketplace and thus represents a component of mySAP.com. mySAP.com consists of four core areas:

◆ The marketplace, an open electronic marketplace for business partners, over which you can develop purchasing, sales, and communications processes that extend beyond individual business.

◆ The workplace, a business portal that provides the user with a browser-based, personalized work environment with all the functions available that he needs to accomplish his daily work.

◆ The mySAP.com business scenarios, which offer role-based business-to-business and business-to-consumer solutions extending beyond the individual business, both through SAP applications and through the applications of other providers.

◆ The Web-based application host, which makes the entire range of mySAP.com solutions available through a fast, cost-efficient group of applications.

New Dimension A product promotion suited to the expanded client demands that promises a great potential for growth. The special solutions guide and optimize the logistics process chain beyond the business boundaries (SAP supply chain management). Operational data are collected and refined into information relevant to decision-making for flexible reaction to changing markets (SAP Business Information Warehouse). Employees of a business can save time and costs by procuring goods and services right from their own desks (Business-to-Business Procurement). Management can make strategic decisions on a solid information base (SAP Business Intelligence Software). These and other initiatives are based on the core functions of the R/3 system but are their own independent solutions.

Pandesic A complete solution of hardware, software, and services for electronic trade on the Internet, jointly developed and marketed by Intel and SAP America. Pandesic is based in large part on the business processes contained in R/3 and directed at small and medium-sized businesses.

Personalizing Adapting software to the individual requirements of a user. Within the workplace concept, personalizing describes an application on the screen of a user who is working with a Web browser and provides a personalized, role-specific view of the total business scenario. This scenario contains the marketplaces, applications, and services that the employer makes available over an intranet or through the Internet.

Portal A new designator for a Web site that serves as the entry point for a structured presentation of search functions. Today, there are portals for a multitude of various communities, as well as Internet portals such as the SAPNet. www.mysap.com, as part of the new product mySAP.com, is likewise a portal.

Role A set of activities that are necessary for a business scenario. Roles such as HR manager or sales representative are oriented toward individual tasks in the business and answer the question: How do I get my job done? Employees can perform various roles in their work. The workplace offers a role-based look at all the functions that a user needs for his business scenario.

SAP InfoDB SAP Information Database; a component of the SAP Knowledge Management Solution. See also *Business intelligence*.

SAP Knowledge Management The SAP solution for a continuous and optimum know-how transfer within the business. It contains the complete SAP training course, multimedia self-learning units, a comprehensive technical encyclopedia, and a special document-management system with which you can also set up and manage your own training courses.

SAP marketing Part of SAP's Customer Relationship Management solution that makes available the tools and functions market strategists need to plan, implement, evaluate, and integrate the marketing program more effectively. SAP marketing provides segment analysis, data-bank-supported market analysis, and market research. With the help of these analytic tools, product and market managers can identify the target markets and evaluate the effect of the marketing programs.

SAP sales Product from the SAP Customer Relationship Management Solution that supports sales and outside services of the business. From the first contact with the customer right up to preparation of the contract, the entire sales process is totally depicted and efficiently planned and controlled. The goal is to reach a high degree of flexibility and a distinct client orientation and commitment.

SAP service A component that makes it possible for employees to resolve clients' problems rapidly and competently. SAP service supports the total service scenarios, including service on the spot, the service activities of the employees in the call center, and self-service on the Internet. All the scenarios emphasize a close integration with the R/3 system. This facilitates the competent and rapid resolution of service incidents; the servicing employee has access to comprehensive customer and service data, and he can directly impact the necessary workflow in the R/3 system.

SAPNet The intranet portal for SAP. SAPNet is also available to partners and clients in a role-specific view. Employees can set up SAPNet individually through the personalizing functions and use it as an access point for employee self-service and procurement functions.

SEM See *Strategic Enterprise Management*.

Solution maps "Road maps" to a tailor-made comprehensive branch system furnishing the business with an overview of industry-specific business processes. Solution maps are put together jointly by user groups, partners, and SAP development teams selected by branch in order to define the requirements of the individual branches. See also *Industry solutions*.

Strategic Enterprise Management A group of tools and processes through which the managerial employees and leadership can initiate value-creation oriented management procedures throughout the business. SAP SEM gives an integrated real-time view of the performance indicators of a business throughout all organizational structures and beyond. The leadership can thus evaluate, as well as enhance, the business value.

Supply chain management The active management of the entire logistics chain (supply chain) from supplier to customer. SAP supports its clients through solutions that integrate the information and decisions from the entire logistics chain in a seamless, automated, and optimized information infrastructure. Within the framework of supply chain management, SAP delivers the applications SAP Advanced Planner and Optimizer (APO) and SAP Logistics Execution System (LES).

TeamSAP An initiative of the SAP that combines its employees with partners, processes, and products with the goal of being able to offer R/3 with better results in a shorter time, at lower costs, and for greater benefit.

ValueSAP ValueSAP is a total approach that integrates the methods, tools, and experience of SAP (such as AcceleratedSAP and TeamSAP) into a universal infrastructure. The goal is to let SAP solutions rapidly contribute creation of value in the business.

Workplace A registered designation for a workplace application of an employee that is tied to a Web browser and provides a personalized and role-specific view of the business administration issues in the business. This includes marketplaces and applications, as well as tasks that are allocated by the employer over the intranet and by other businesses over the Internet. See also *mySAP.com*.

XML Extensible markup language. A data format for structured data exchange over the Web. XML itself is not a descriptive language like HTML, but rather a type of meta-language with which you can generate other specialized languages. XML documents are increasingly employed to make collaboration between businesses possible by the exchange of business documents over the Internet.

Index

B

Internet *(continued)*
   misuse of, 231
   multidimensional information, 243
   paradigm shift and, 91–92
   planning data, integrating, 212
   price transparency of, 210–211
   procurement development on, 202
   production changes and, 202
   R/3 architecture and, 204
   real applications and, 39
   real-time information and, 38
   SAPNet, 32
   service on, 224–225
   social opportunities, 244–245
   software demonstrations, 226–227
   strategy of SAP, 247
   technology of, 154
   users of, 239
interpreter concept, 64–65
interpreters, 16
I2 planning system, 132
ITS (Internet Transaction Server), 115

J

Jaguar, 162
Japan, 34–36
   R/3 in, 250
Java, 82, 115–116, 147, 188
   development of, 117
   touch-screen front ends in, 115
J.D. Edwards, 24
Jessen, Professor, 61
Jobs, Steve, 2
John Deere, 11, 20
   initiating relationship with, 248

K

Kagermann, Henning, 129, 182, 184,
   197, 229–230, 252
Karlsruhe, University of, 1–2, 54
   departure from, 5
   process engineering, 174
Kemira, 21, 24

Kenya, R/3 in, 50
Kienzle, 189
Kilroy, Jim, 46
Korea, 35, 48

L

laptop computers
   business scenarios and, 143
   data availability, 100
   R/3 system on, 78
Leidig, Klaus-Dieter, 191–192
lexical knowledge, 63
libraries, Internet and, 102
Lions, Sir John, 160
logistics businesses, 214–215
Lost City, South Africa, 49
Lotus, 33, 190

M

McCormick and Dodge, 26
McKinsey, 217
McNeally, Scott, 7
mainframes
   expense of, 86
   R/3 system on, 73
Manager **magazine,** 251
Mandela, Nelson, 4–5
Manugistics, 132
marketing
   to end users, 156–157
   in United States, 27–28
marketplace, mySAP.com, 212–215,
   234–236
marketplace systems, 238–239
materials, transporting, 214–215
Matheis, Dieter, 195
mathematics-oriented information
   scientists, 166
mechanical engineering, 174
memory storage, 101
menus, role-specific, 206–207
message-processing regions, 75
meta-concepts, 120

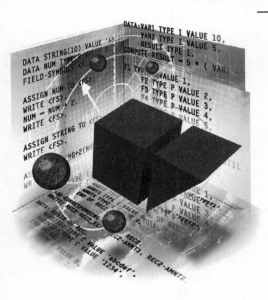